Retake Your Safe Space

the art of self encouragement

Henry C.Ohakah

Retake Your Safe Space

The art of self encouragement

Published by: Spirit Wind

Scripture quotations are from the HOLY BIBLE, NEW KING JAMES VERSION except where otherwise stated. Emphasis within scripture is the author's own.

ISBN: 979-8-4916-5269-3

We want to hear from you. Please send your comments about this book to us on the contact details at the last page. Thank you.

Dedication

To my greatest credentials and most powerful prayer force, my best friend Anita and my three anointed children Somtochi, Chimdumebi and Chilemeze. You sacrifice daily to allow me to pursue my dreams and visions of bringing the healing world and touching a dying world.

Endorsements

We live in a world that seems, almost by default, to set us up for failure. We are compelled to have targets to reach, goals to score, records to break. Whilst these may appear be worthy goals, that drive us on to greater achievements, and can leave our souls barren and broken.

In his book, Henry C Ohakah, unpacks the real secret of Success and Advancement and inspires and motivate the reader to rediscover and capture the tools for a life that is full and overflowing with purpose, peace, and power

At the start we must recognise our own inability to succeed without the Power and Presence of the Living God in our lives. Accessing and outworking God's provision and purposes, releases a confidence and a deep security into all we are and all that we do.

Secondly, we learn how we must shake ourselves free from the shackles of guilt and the fear of failure that so easy consume our thoughts, and rise in grace and faith for our future, to then become the person we were designed and crafted to be.

Thirdly, we are given tools to help us reflect and remember our own journey of faith - to reveal the depth of God's faithfulness and his ability to bring to completion the work he has started both in us and through us.

-Rev. Adrian Dexter *MTh*
Senior Pastor, Liberty Church
Rotherham, United Kingdom

My friend and co-labourer in the things of God, Henry Ohakah, has in this book articulated the need to understand that we have a "Safe Place" in God, and it is available now. Retaking that place is the theme of "Retake Your Safe Place" and is filled with the insight necessary to do just that. In a world set for opposition, this reveals the light of God's word and what we have through Him: A "Safe Place".

Jesus said in John 14:3 *"And if I go and prepare a place for you, I will come again, and receive you unto myself; that where I am, there ye may be also."* The place He prepared is not just about heaven but His Kingdom. The place He prepared is a place of authority and peace that we can have right now. Realizing your "Safe Place" can be a very present reality is a life-changing revelation. Henry exposes us to the knowledge that God has, through the success of the Cross, given us everything we need to succeed. We truly can be more than overcomers.

Henry has done a magnificent job pointing out through the scriptures the ability to know there is a "Safe Place", and how to get there as well as keep it. The enemy is good at what he does and according to 2 Cor 4:4, works at blinding the minds of the world to the truth God has for them. And in many cases the church as well. That truth is a truth David understood, self-encouragement. The ability to look past the circumstances life throws at us and move forward is a God-given ability. Choose to use it!

There is power in your words. The scripture says the power of life and death is in the tongue. Henry points to that power and the ability we have when we choose to affirm and proclaim all that God has done for and through us.

There will always be challenges, battles, storms, and circumstances that will try and bring discouragement and despair, but there is a place in God! Jesus prepared it just for you. It is your "Safe Place". Choose to take it back!

-Pastor Jack Williams
Founder/Senior Pastor, Covenant Life Fellowship & Boerne Covenant Life Texas, USA Founder, Mission Initiative Bible Program (MIBP) (two schools in India & one in Pakistan)

When my friend and brother asked me to write this recommendation I was honoured and considered it a privilege. Without hesitation my answer was yes, thank you very much. I took the decision not to read the nook in its entirety before righting this. Why? I look forward to reading it along with everyone else who will be fortunate to hear the words of a considerate and insightful man. Also, I suppose, the decision was a compliment to my friend. I trust his writing will indeed be considered and insightful as ai know this to be the man that he is.

The title of the book, 'Take back your safe space', and the introduction to the book, which I have read in advance is enough to catch one's curiosity and whet the appetite for the subject at hand.

We are in a world and a time in history when we could easily ask, and probably do, if there is any such thing as privacy? Do we have a safe space where we are not being watched, photographed, or recorded on someone's phone with or without our knowledge and permission?

It is a challenging time. It is equally as challenging a time to be a Christian in this world. Again, we are watched, scrutinised, and held up for all the world to see, and tear us down at first opportunity. That is before we look at the way Christians behave toward each other in the same fashion.

Much like the subject matter my friend writes of here in this book, people react to so many things in so many ways. Often, not in the way they would hope to be reacted to, or to be treated in any given situation. Human thinking, emotions the standards we hold people to are very curious at times to say the least. That is why it is so important to have a safe place.
The only safe place we truly have that cannot be invaded by humanity is the mind which the Lord himself has given to us. Even that place will find itself under attack, invaded by our one and only true enemy, the enemy of our God and our soul, Satan, the deceiver, the liar, the prince of darkness and the Lord of this world.

When my friend talks of self-encouragement he speaks with insight. Of course, he does not speak of the 'Self' that is self-reliant or self-indulgent. He is not denying the need for the Lord. It is in our self that we must make the decision not to hand victory in any moment to Satan. To achieve this, sometimes, in our more vulnerable moments, we must fight through the human instinct of pity. We must not allow Satan to convince us that the world is against us, that we are abandoned. Even if that appears to be the case, we know that the Lord our God will never leave us nor forsake us. It is often right at that lowest of moments as we desperately cry out to our God, he will remind us of, or send a friend in Christ to our aide!

But above all things, the one thing Satan cannot take from us is that ability to remind oneself of the Lord God almighty who had been with us throughout our life. That same Lord who has delivered us through many trials. Try as he might, Satan cannot stop us from recalling, and therefore being encouraged in the Lord. Ready now for this next attack, this next test whatever it may be.

Whatever it may well be, it is too an extent irrelevant, because the same Lord who delivered through all the others is right by our side. He does not change and does not abandon us.

In the relatively short time, I have known my friend I have known him to be a considered and insightful man. I know that he, like all of us has felt the frustrations, pain, and anxieties of this life. I know he has felt alone in the battle. Yet, I say that I have never heard him complain nor speak in reflection with any bitterness. Yes, he has spoken with a broken heart at the recollection of the will and word of the Lord being secondary to man's ways and thoughts.

I know my friend to be a man who listens, reflects, and considers and falls before the Lord God in all things. I wait in anticipation, with that knowledge, to read his thoughts on this subject matter.
There is no substitute for experience, Henry has that. There is no hope like the hope of the Lord Jesus shining before us. Henry has that shining brightly, with love and passion from his soul.
Like David, as we read in 1 Samuel 30. He does not react impulsively but turns to the Lord and those whom he considers friends in the Lord. This can only make for a blessing of a book filled with lessons to be learned by those with the humility and desire to grow in our Lord.

Satan will try to put us down, he meets us in the battle ground of our mind, this is his playground. Let him try to turn the light of Christ Jesus of and make it his dark room. Simply remind him the light has overcome the darkness and the darkness cannot and will not conquer the light of Christ in your life!

Simply remind him that he is indeed a liar, and you are a child of the truth. The truth is that the power and authority of Christ is in you. The one power and authority that he cannot overcome, and from which he flees.
Simply remind him of his future. Remember your past through the eyes of the Lord. Your sins are gone for he has taken them. You are a conqueror who has overcome many attacks from Satan because the Lord has carried you through every battle. Take back, reinforce your safe space with the encouragement of the Lord and he will carry you forward toward glory.
It is my great pleasure to commend these thoughts and this book to you in the name of the Lord.

-Pastor Peter McCool
Pastor, South Sheffield Evangelical Church
Sheffield, United Kingdom

I am deeply honoured to recommend this book by Rev. Henry Ohakah. At a time when the world is facing the most unsettled times in her history, the need for individuals to understand God's plans for living a fulfilled life in all circumstances is highly important.
The author stresses the need to take personal responsibility by drawing close to God in recognition that He alone can give us the Power above all powers. In Him we are able to gain stability and find encouragement through all challenging life circumstances. Every new day gives us an opportunity to reflect on the fact that the present is an indication of His Faithfulness in times past.

According to the author this can be a very strong source of confidence to face our impeding challenges in life. This and many other powerful principles are passionately shared in this book, and I am very hopeful that all readers will find it most edifying.

-Dr. David Oloke
Senior Pastor, Lifegate Church
Walsall, United Kingdom

Each one of us is born to fulfil a purpose here on earth. No one came by mistake irrespective of how he was conceived and where he was born. Also, each one of us can achieve our purpose and live a fulfilled life wherever we are living in. However, there is a place we all can flourish in, it's our safe place, we must seek to be planted there. The safe place for a believer is God's will concerning him. You must find out what God's will is concerning you, insist on it, and refuse to be dislodged from there. God's will for you is the place of your deliverance, your victory, success, healing, and genuine satisfaction.

The evil one, Satan, will fight to hinder you from taking your safe place, he enjoys your misery. His threefold mission is to steal, kill and destroy (John 10:10) however, the Bible says in 1 Timothy 6:12 to "fight the good fight of faith…." You must be ready to fight to win. The devil will only succeed when the believer does not fight the good fight of faith. One of the devil's strategies is to keep the believer in the dark of what belongs to him in Christ Jesus. You must seek knowledge, seek to know what God says about you. Knowledge is very powerful, and the knowledge of who you are, what belongs to you in your relationship with Jesus and what you can become is life transforming; Henry Ohakah has beautifully brought all these truth to light in this book.

Jesus said in John 8:32 "you shall know the truth, and the truth shall make you free." You are who God says you are. You can do what God says you can do. You can become what is God's plan for you. That's your truth; everything to the contrary is false. The Bible says in Ephesians 1:18 "The eyes of your understanding being enlightened; that ye may know what is the hope of his calling, and what the riches of the glory of his inheritance in the saints".

Henry Ohakah has done a fantastic work in writing the book 'Retake Your Safe Space'. The book is filled with divine wisdom, and revelation knowledge. It's filled with the tools that can help you retake what the devil stole and become victorious in challenging situations. It is well written, easy to grasp and apply to everyday life. 'Retake Your safe space' is very empowering, I unreservedly recommend it to you. Read the pages prayerfully, don't keep it to yourself, pass it round. Happy reading.

-Pastor Musa Bako
Senior Pastor, Victory Assembly Sheffield
Assistant Regional pastor @RCCG UK

In all the earth, the greatest source of encouragement is the Word of God. And one of my most favourite scripture by which I am encouraged are the profound words that God originally spoke to Joshua when this successor of Moses desperately needed encouragement to overcome his fears and feelings of inadequacy. God said to Joshua, *"Have I not commanded you? Be strong and courageous. Do not be frightened, and do not be dismayed, for the LORD your God is with you wherever you go.""* (Joshua 1:9, ESV)

Why is it critical that we learn the art of self-encouragement and be able to re-take our safe space?

One does not need to look too far but to the invasive and sudden nature of discouragement along with the fact that prolonged feelings of discouragement can be deleterious to our emotional state and, indeed, debilitate one's life in general. It is true that life is full of uncertainties and can at times be downright tough. Life is littered with storms, barriers, and stumbling blocks. Saved or not, the truth is that we will all face many challenges in this life and experience some discouragements along the way. Yet, it is the will of God for us to be strong and courageous, and not be dismayed by the storms of life.

The feeling of discouragement may come upon one quite suddenly. They may arise from some physical, emotional, or spiritual issues one is dealing with. Some will press us much harder than most even to the point of depression and despair. But, in times like these, it is helpful to recall the words of the psalmist saying, *"You prepare a table before me in the presence of my enemies..."* (Psalm 23:5). How reassuring to know that if God has prepared such a banquet of life's blessings for you, He will also give you grace to enjoy every blessing on that table despite the enemy lurking about looking for a victim to devour.

Some people are disillusioned because they feel that being a believer should immune them from pain and suffering. Such wrong thinking is the reason many cannot "encourage themselves in the Lord." They doubt God when adversity strikes. The Prophet Elijah, a mighty man of God who prayed and God answered by sending down fire from heaven, faced such a moment of disillusion and loss of enthusiasm. John the Baptist did too, resulting in him questioning if Jesus was really the Messiah.

No one is immune from discouragement, but ultimately, we must learn to retake our safe space and not allow lack of encouragement to become the bane of our existence. We must deal with discouraging situations with right thinking and right attitude. For example, when Jesus said, *"I have said these things to you, that in me you may have peace. In the world you will have tribulation. But take heart; I have overcome the world."* (John 16:33, ESV), he gives us a new way of dealing with discouraging moments in life. He immediately tells us not to have peace in Him and not to see adversities as strange occurrences or reason to doubt God. Then He tells us to "take heart" or "be encouraged." The message being that He who has overcome the world will also overcome for us in the specific situations of our daily lives.

Reflecting on a particular time of great difficulty during his ministry, the Apostle Paul wrote:

> *"For we do not want you to be unaware, brothers, of the affliction we experienced in Asia. For we were so utterly burdened beyond our strength that we despaired of life itself. Indeed, we felt that we had received the sentence of death. But that was to make us rely not on ourselves but on God who raises the dead. He delivered us from such a deadly peril, and he will deliver us. On him we have set our hope that he will deliver us again."* (2 Corinthians 1:8–10, ESV)

In this juxtaposition of utter despair and hope in God, Paul shows us that no matter how discouraged one feels, the way of escape is to *"rely not on ourselves but on God who raises the dead."*

Anything that can cause one to lose confidence or enthusiasm, even for a moment, can be the source of significant feeling of discouragement. Such things are potent because they generate feelings that trick our minds and distort reality to make us feel helpless and, therefore, compel us to give up and not fulfil our potential.

Winston Churchill is famously quoted as having said that, *"Success is the ability to go from one failure to another with no loss of enthusiasm."* And the suggestion here being that to make progress in life, one must learn how to move past discouraging experiences and doubts and move forward with enthusiasm and hope.

In this book, Ohaka has highlighted the saying that the world seems to have been *"designed to make you fail"*. Life can certainly feel that way sometimes, as if a series of events have conspired to go awry all at once to undermine you at every turn. And the question becomes, how do you regain and sustain the enthusiasm for forward momentum? Where would you find encouragement when even those you would usually turn to are themselves in similar need?

A helpful definition from the Dictionary of Biblical Themes describes "discouragement" as, *"A sense of unhappiness arising from a loss of confidence in one's own abilities, in the reliability of God, or in the power of the gospel."* In addition, Warren Wiersbe succinctly observes that, *"The remedy for discouragement is the word of God. When you feed your heart and mind with its truth, you regain your perspective and find renewed strength."*

This book, "The Art of Self-Encouragement," recognizes the crisis that a lack of encouragement can create in a person's life and seeks to challenge its readers to embrace the grace of God who is our encourager by turning to God for help like David did. As the Psalmist testified, *"God is our refuge and strength, a very present help in trouble times"* (Psalm 46:1).

Confronted with the distressing and discouraging events of Ziklag (1 Samuel 30:1-6) and being unable to count on the help of his close associates, who were themselves equally traumatized by the devastation of their homes, David wisely made the decision not to give in to the overwhelming emotions of despair. He made a choice to turn his attention away from what little he could do by his own power and sought encouragement in God, the One with whom all things are possible.

In God, David found the ultimate encourager as we all must. And by his example in turning to God for encouragement, every believer is made to understand that it is possible to encounter extremely tough times and still find the motivation, courage, and strength to plough ahead even as everything around says that you cannot. We find that encouragement when we turn to God. We can encourage ourselves in the Lord saying,

> *"I lift up my eyes to the hills. From where does my help come? My help comes from the LORD, who made heaven and earth. He will not let your foot be moved; he who keeps you will not slumber."* (Psalm 121:1–3, ESV).

And according to Jeremy Taylor, a 17th century British Anglican Bishop and writer, *"It is impossible for that man to despair who remembers that his Helper is omnipotent."*

The God and Father of our Lord Jesus Christ is *"the God of endurance and encouragement"* (Romans 15:5). He encourages the believer through *"the encouragement of the Scriptures"* (v.4). And it is the will of God that His word resides in the believer richly, the goal being that we permit God's word to speak expressly to every aspect of our lives ministering encouragement when one is required.

Furthermore, God has given His Holy Spirit to those who believe not merely to dwell *"with"* them, but crucially, *"within"* them. And the Spirit of God lives within the believer in His capacity as "Helper" (from the original word "*Parakletos*"), which also means *"Encourager"*.

The bottom line is that God has given mankind the psychological capacity to endure those really discouraging aspects of life's ups and downs. And, in Christ, one receives the spiritual resources to overcome them and thrive despite them. Along with the word of God and the presence of the Holy Spirit, we also have the privilege of prayer and praise, both efficacious in accessing divine help, strength, and motivation.

The profession and testimony of a person who has made the Lord his or her encourager will be no different from these declarations of scriptures:

> *"The LORD is my strength and my shield; in him my heart trusts, and I am helped; my heart exults, and with my song I give thanks to him"* (Psalm 28:7, ESV).
> *"Blessed is the man who trusts in the LORD, whose trust is the LORD"* (Jeremiah 17:7, ESV),
> *"for the LORD will be your confidence and will keep your foot from being caught."* (Proverbs 3:26, ESV).

In his moment of deep discouragements and despair, David chose to walk by faith, not by sight. He encouraged himself, not by focusing on his own abilities (which would only discourage him more for how inadequate they were) and not by looking to the people around him (which would have been a distraction for they were ill-equipped to help). By faith, David turned instead to *"the God of encouragement"* - the God who can infuse the weary with courage and give strength to the weak.

Understanding this spiritual principle of encouraging oneself in the Lord opens a whole new and wonderful world of possibilities for dealing with difficult times. It is a world in which the believer living by faith, lives a life empowered by the power of God.

If one seeks a standard portrait of a person who encourages himself in the Lord, Romans 15:13 paints a good one: *"May the God of hope fill you with all joy and peace in believing, so that by the power of the Holy Spirit you may abound in hope."* A person who puts their trust in God is encouraged! Abounding in hope, they have a good expectation of the future always, and are thus filled with joy and peace no matter which way the wind blows.

In a world that is more connected than ever before in human history, one would expect that the corresponding sense of community will multiply encouragement, yet it seems, anecdotally, that the reverse is the case. People are more lonely, depressed, and distressed than ever before. Even Christians are caught up in that wave of social media induced sense of inadequacy and discouragement.

Rev. Ohaka has written an especially useful and timely book in which we are reminded of the value of self-encouragement and challenged to practice it by finding our encouragement in the God of all comfort. His observation that it often appears that "the world is designed to make you fail" reinforces the urgent need to look to God and not to the world for encouragement.

"Why worry," writes Karen Mikhai, *"when you can pray? Why have fears when you know God hears? And why think of failure when we know through God success is for sure?"* And in Proverbs 24:10 we are challenged to make the Lord our strength, for *"If you faint in the day of adversity, your strength is small."*

God who promised to work in us to desire and to do His good pleasure, has also assured us that He will never allow to us go through any challenges that we are unable to bear. He will never abandon us or let us walk alone, and He is able to inspire confidence and courage in us and stimulate hope and enthusiasm in us through the encouragement of scriptures.

An important key to encouraging oneself in the Lord is to never doubt God or become weary of asking for His help. Having trust in God, the Father of our Lord Jesus Christ, is critical to our overall success in life and to our victory over the causes and consequences of discouragement. The need to be intentional in turning to God for encouragement cannot be overstated. As someone said, any sign of discouragement, "*ought to be the first indication that it is time to pray.*"
And the man or woman who has learned to turn to the Lord for encouragement will always be found singing with the Psalmist, *"I am still confident of this: I will see the goodness of the Lord in the land of the living."* (Psalm 27:13, NIV).

Be strong in the Lord and in the power of His might for there is indeed encouragement in Christ. Discover it, press into it by faith, and re-take your safe space – the place of encouragement in the Lord.

-Pastor Victor Ubani
Founder / Senior Pastor - Sure Word International Church
London, United Kingdom

Table of Contents

Foreword

There was a time in my life when I felt overwhelmed by anxiety. The worry was mostly caused by financial pressure and by a nagging fear of failure. I tried my best to put into words my fears and frustrations, but my prayers were basically a series of groans. So many doubts assaulted my mind: *Will the money run out? Did I follow God's plan correctly? Did I even hear God in the first place?*

Then a clear picture popped into my mind, and I knew it was an impression from the Holy Spirit. I saw an aerial view of the street where I lived in the suburbs of Atlanta, Georgia, during the 1970s. I saw a huge semi-truck parked in front of my house. I asked the Lord what He was showing me.

My mind was flooded with memories of what God did in my life when I lived in that house in 1976. I experienced a divine intervention in the fall of that year, just weeks before I was to leave home for college. I was filled with the Holy Spirit that September, and my life was radically redirected. The Lord saved me from following my own selfish plans, and He put me on the right path.

I asked the Lord why He was showing me a semi-truck parked in front of my house. He spoke to my heart: "It was when you lived in that house in 1976 that I brought you a huge load of my grace and mercy."

I immediately thanked Him for all He had done for me. I was reminded of Psalm 103:4, which says in the International Children's Bible: "He saves my life from the grave. He loads me with love and mercy."

But then I saw another picture in my mind, and this time, the semi-truck was parked in front of the house where I live now, in 2021. The Lord said: "I am bringing you another load of my mercy and grace." And I was reminded of Ephesians 1:7-8 (MEV), which says we have redemption and forgiveness "according to the riches of His grace, which He lavished on us."

Again, I had to pour out my heart in thanksgiving. God's grace doesn't just come once. His grace is not rationed in small quantities. The word "lavish" means "to cause to abound and overflow." What happened at Calvary did not end there. He opened a fountain then, but it continues to gush today. He brings His grace to us in truckloads, and then He brings more!

Perhaps you have wondered if God's grace toward you is running out. Maybe you thought He was tired of your mistakes, upset about your doubts or frustrated with your inconsistency. Maybe you wondered if you misheard His divine direction. Maybe you even worried that He had disqualified you.

You can be encouraged today. His grace never stopped. We have received "grace upon grace" (John 1:16) and "the abundance of grace" (Rom. 5:17).

Jesus told the apostle Paul: "My grace is sufficient for you" (2 Cor. 12:9). God will supply you with all the grace you need if you simply humble yourself and acknowledge your need for Him. James 4:6 tells us that God "gives more grace" when we come to Him in humility.

When my friend Henry Ohakah sent me the manuscript of his book, my mind was flooded with memories of the promises God has given me over the years. Some of them have not been fulfilled yet—and I can be tempted to give up and stop believing for their fulfillment. You may be in that place of discouragement right now. But I believe this book will be like a truckload of grace, pulling up in front of your house to deliver fresh faith and expectation.

Truly, it is time to dream again. It is time to believe again. As you ponder the miracle of abundant grace, remember this:

His grace delivers you from your past. You should thank God daily that you aren't where you would be if you hadn't met Christ. You might not even be alive today if it weren't for His merciful intervention! Be grateful that He broke the power of sin in your life, forgave you for your many wrong choices and freed you from guilt. You are a walking miracle because of what Jesus already did for you.

His grace empowers you for the present. Even though you often feel weak, and you know you are a flawed vessel, God's grace works through you supernaturally. His Spirit lives in you. His anointing is a precious treasure that flows out of imperfect saints. When Jesus told Paul, "My grace is sufficient for you," He added, "for My strength is made perfect in weakness" (2 Cor. 12:9). Quit trying to be perfect; just relax, knowing that He is working in you.

His grace guides you into your future. We all reach moments when we feel we've hit a wall. Elijah saw God's fire fall on Mount Carmel, but then he found himself in a cave of fear and depression. He even thought of ending his life. But then he heard the still, small voice of God again. He received such a fresh outpouring of grace that he outran Ahab and saw the promised downpour of rain.

This is not a time to give up. I pray that this book will rekindle your dreams and reset your weakened faith. Spiritual warfare may be intense, and you may be painfully aware of your own flaws. But God's grace is greater than the devil, his demons, and your mistakes. Open your eyes, and you will see a truckload of grace heading your way.

-J. Lee Grady

Director, The Mordecai Project
Author of Set My Heart on Fire, 10 Lies the Church Tells Women, Follow Me, and
other books

Introduction

There is a popular saying that "the world is designed to make you fail". Somewhere else I read that "the world is setting you up to fail". Truth be told, I don't find that hard to believe. Society creates so much hostile atmosphere that it takes strong will and self-encouragement to go through the daily huddles that come our way. The world's governments and their economy also follow in this direction.

I heard the story of a minister who was being watched by a little boy while he was building a garden trellis. As he was pounding away, he noticed that the little boy was watching him very keenly. The youngster didn't say a word, so the preacher kept on working, thinking the lad would leave. But he didn't. Pleased at the thought that his work was being admired, the pastor finally said, "Well, son, trying to pick up some pointers on gardening?" "No," he replied. "I'm just waiting to hear what a preacher says when he hits his thumb with a hammer."

That boy was watching to see how the preacher would respond to pain. How he would deal with pain. How he would handle hurt. The world is a lot like that little boy. It watches how we as children of God will act when faced with suffering, injustice, and unfairness. The world expects to see anger, resentment, bitterness, and rage.

As a Christian you may be reluctant to admit that the world is designed to make you fail, but before you dismiss this notion look at the story of David and his men in 1 Samuel 30:1-6. He had lost everything that had meaning in his life. His home was burned, his wife, children and belongings were taken, don't forget that David was a leader, so the loss of his men's families was also heavy on him.

When faced with such heavy discouragement, most people will start having suicidal thoughts, some may slip into depression. Some of us may even start looking for whom to blame for our misfortunes. On top of all his losses, his men turned on him. they wanted to stone him. "…But David encouraged himself in The Lord his God". There is something about this statement that tickles my fancy. If there was anyone who spoke encouraging words to David at this point, the Bible did not mention. This is why I tell people that the greatest prophet of your life is 'you'. The best motivational speaker who can make a meaningful impact in your life is yourself.

Self-love, affirmations, positive speaking, proclamations all reinforce self-encouragement. Self-motivation is always the most powerful kind of motivation. You hear others speak words of encouragement to you, but the day you decide to encourage yourself, you begin to heal and take control of your environment.

Before now there was a song sung about David and Saul,

"Saul has slain his thousands, and David his tens of thousands."

Also remember that this same David killed a lion, a bear, and the Philistine giant Goliath. You'd think David will encourage himself with these feats. But David encouraged himself in The Lord his God. David did not stop there; he went ahead to seek the face of the Lord. No wonder when he inquired of the Lord, God told him to

"pursue, for you shall surely overtake them and without fail recover all."

Self-encouragement can be the most powerful arsenal in fighting all of life's battles, especially when done in the Lord.

Some of the things you will learn in this book:
- Recognize the higher power. The Bible is not a collection of poems. When it says, *"I can do all things through Christ who strengthens me"* (Philippians 4:13) brother Paul wasn't trying to be poetic. You have the innate abilities to surmount every obstacle that comes your way, all you have to do is recognize that you have no strength of your own. Your strength comes from your creator, the Lord Almighty.
- Remember all He has done for you and through you in the past. When you are in doubt, remember what God had done for you in the past, remember what He has done through you in the past. I am imagining that when the Amalekites took David's family from Ziklag, he thought of how God had used him to slay numerous beasts, how God had led him into battles and he came out victorious, suddenly strength came into his spirit.
- Turn to God when you are facing any challenge. *"Then David said to Abiathar the priest, the son of Ahimelek, "bring me the ephod."* Abiathar brought it to him, and

David inquired of the LORD" [1 Sam 30:7-8a]. When you encourage yourself, your spirit becomes energized, but when you don't seek God's direction and guidance, your strength will definitely fail you. Form a habit of asking God for His directions regularly.

The ultimate truth is that God has given us all it takes to succeed in this life. He created us with not just the willpower but also the tools to win all life's battles. So even if the world is setting us up to fail, we have been given the right tools to succeed.

"Put on the whole armour of God, that you may be able to stand against the wiles of the devil." Ephesians 6:11

Understand that the devil doesn't fight you physically. Your mind is the battlefield, so keep fighting your battles with the weapon of self-encouragement.

My desire is that by reading this book, you would make a strong resolve to retake your safe space. Take back your inheritance, your possession, and your mental health. God sees your confusion; He sees that you really don't understand why you are going through situations. You might even have thought about giving up on God, you don't think that He sees what you are thinking.

I want to see you become a person ready to face difficulties in life with grace and inner strength and may this book give you hope for your struggles.

Chapter One
The Power of Self Encouragement

We've all known discouragement to varying degrees. I strongly believe that you have had a bad day before. These things do happen. Every one of us faces discouraging situations no matter who we are or where we live, the only thing different might be the way we react and how we manage the experiences and what we make out of them. Even the giants in the faith, such as the apostle Paul, knew times of deep despair and was completely overwhelmed that he even had some suicidal thoughts.

"For we do not want you to be ignorant, brethren, of our trouble which came to us in Asia: that we were burdened beyond measure, above strength, so that we despaired even of life." 1 Corinthians 1:8.

The feeling of stress is common but what feels stressful to one person may be motivating to someone else. Some people are quick to overcome it while others take a while or succumb to it and give up. Experts often talk about the 'fight or flight' response. In fact, life's demands can bring us stress. These could be work, our relationships, money, and many other things, and when you feel weighed down, it can get in the way of how you sort out your daily demands or how you think and behave and can even affect how your physical body works. The way you react to family and friends could be impacted as well.

We are living in a time when many people's emotional status is messed up. There is so much fear, hopelessness, and discouragement. There is little we can do to prevent what might come our way, but there are many things we can do to take charge under the power of the Holy Spirit. Learning from what Martin Luther said, I can tell you that you might not keep the birds of sadness from flying over your head, but you can keep them from building a nest in your hair.

On one occasion, Martin Luther was overwhelmed with depression. It didn't seem to lift despite the appeals of family and friends. Finally, his wife, Katie, put on the black garments of a widow in mourning. When Luther noticed, he asked her who had died. She replied that God in heaven must have died, judging from Luther's demeanour. His depression lifted instantly as he laughed and kissed his wise wife. Everyone can get stressed up from time to time, but you can find ways to overcome stress and prevent it from turning into something that keeps you down forever.

A friend once told this story; Once upon a time, he said, the devil put his tools up for sale, each marked with their price. The products included stealing, pride, lying, hatred, jealousy, lust, deceit, and so on. And just at the corner of his shop was a very harmless looking little well-worn tool and this one was marked with an unbelievably high price. A customer was shocked and asked, "what is this tool and why is it ridiculously high?", the devil replied and told him that the tool is called discouragement "and it is this high because it is more useful to me than the others", he boasted. "I can pry open a person's heart with that when I can't get near to them with anything else. It's so badly worn because I use it on almost everyone, since few people know it belongs to me," the devil concluded. Discouragement is a terrible disease and a very powerful weapon in the hand of the enemy of our soul. It is very expensive in the devil's market because you pay with your life.

Discouragement is a personal decision. You need to make a conscious decision not to be discouraged. This is why sometimes believers are a wonder to the unsaved. We have joy even when there is no natural reason to do so. Joy, I have always said, is not the same as happiness. Happiness is just at the soul realm, but joy is supernatural. No one can discourage you except you decide to discourage yourself. It is a personal decision. It is sad but true that many people wage war against themselves. Many people downgrade themselves continually with their mouths. Whenever the devil wants to box you to a corner, encourage yourself in the Lord. Discouraged people believe that life is a failure.

To be quite honest with you, I think discouragement has killed more people than sicknesses and diseases. Discouraged people abort victory by their actions and the way they treat themselves during difficult times. They see victory coming but never live to celebrate because they give up prematurely. They borrow problem from the future. They are worried about tomorrow even though they do not know what will happen tomorrow. They borrow the problems of the future and transfer them to the present. This does not make sense at all. Tomorrow is too early to worry about. When we are discouraged, we actually fail to give ourselves enough time to heal from the ugly experiences of past mistakes and we make up our minds that perhaps the Lord has gone on a holiday or is taking a nap.

The Grasshopper Mentality

The Lord once said to me that what many people need is to be delivered from "the grasshopper mentality." What is grasshopper mentality, you may ask? It is the mentality you have when you believe that you are not able.

In Numbers chapter 13, the Lord told Moses to send spies to the Promised Land. Representatives from every tribe in the land of Israel. They went off on their espionage but after more than one month of their assignment, all the men brought back a bad report except one man called Caleb who stood his ground against discouragement. This is what they reported back to Moses and Aaron and all the congregation of the children of Israel,

"Then they told him and said: "We went to the land where you sent us. It truly flows with milk and honey, and this is its fruit. Nevertheless, the people who dwell in the land are strong; the cities are fortified and very large; moreover, we saw the descendants of Anak there."

"Then Caleb quieted the people before Moses, and said, "Let us go up at once and take possession, for we are well able to overcome it." But the men who had gone up with him said, "We are not able to go up against the people, for they are stronger than we." There we saw the giants (the descendants of Anak came from the giants); and we were like grasshoppers in our own sight, and so we were in their sight." Numbers 13:27-28,30-31,33

The grasshopper mentality makes you see yourself as inferior, it makes you give up even before trying. Did you notice that the men saw themselves as grasshoppers! No other person saw them this way. Oh, how that feeling of insecurity has knocked down many people. Feeling intimidated is very common with people with a grasshopper mentality. They always feel anxious around other people. They feel they are not smart enough or cool enough. When you do this, any small critical comment can often send you into a spiral of depression and self-hate and any slight sign of rejection or exclusion will make you feel totally miserable. The next time you have these feelings, remember this, it's you, not him or her! And can I shock you? Other people are nervous too! My advice would be to care more about what you think of yourself. Get rooted in your own value system. Stop changing or bending yourself depending on who is around. And one more thing, never ever compare yourself with anyone. It is unavoidable that some people are going to be better than you at some things where they spend the most time practicing or where they have a natural talent. But do you know that sometimes these people neglect other areas of life where you are actually better than they are? But a grasshopper mentality prevents you from viewing yourself through your own area of strength and that's why I said other people might be nervous too. You are not inferior, you are not superior, you are simply you. Your value comes from your uniqueness.

Apostle Paul criticised the false teachers who were trying to prove their goodness by comparing themselves with others rather than with God's standards.

"For we dare not class ourselves or compare ourselves with those who commend themselves. But they, measuring themselves by themselves, and comparing themselves among themselves, are not wise." 2 Corinthians 10:12

To "compare themselves" in the original language can be translated "copying one another." God has made each of us unique and given us spiritual gifts that are unique. It is never wise to copy or compare yourself to another believer. Pride will result if we see ourselves as better than someone else, or discouragement if we see ourselves as less valuable than someone else. We don't live by comparison to others but by Christ's life in us.

The other day I was discussing with my wife how it is that many young people today have feelings of self-doubt and inferiority simply because of someone else's social media post, and I remember a few years ago speaking at a national youth conference in Nigeria and telling them that people only present distorted versions of themselves on social media, we don't need a Facebook post to judge how happy someone's life has been. At best, these things are only distorted posts that edited all the sad, boring, and plain parts out. Don't fall for it. The same things could also be said about TV and magazines, they send images of the most successful, attractive, and wealthy people in the world straight into your home, or so we think.

In reality, all impossible situations are opportunities in disguise.

No one can discourage you except you decide to discourage yourself, so take a conscious decision not to be discouraged. Take a decision this moment to always encourage yourself in the Lord, then you can hear Him clearly. Encourage yourself in the Lord and render thanksgiving to Him. Tell Him you appreciate His blessings and faithfulness. Decide that circumstances will not enslave your soul no matter what.

I will like us to learn a lesson or two from David in the Bible. Come with me to 1 Samuel 30:1-6.

"Now it happened, when David and his men came to Ziklag, on the third day, that the Amalekites had invaded the South and Ziklag, attacked Ziklag and burned it with fire, ² and had taken captive the women and those who were there, from small to great; they did not kill anyone, but carried them away and went their way. ³ So David and his men came to the city, and there it was, burned with fire; and their wives, their sons, and their daughters had been taken captive. ⁴ Then David and the people who were with him lifted up their voices and wept, until they had no more power to weep. ⁵ And David's two wives, Ahinoam the Jezreelitess, and Abigail the widow of Nabal the Carmelite, had been taken captive. ⁶ Now David was greatly distressed, for the people spoke of stoning him, because the soul of all the people was grieved, every man for his sons and his daughters. But David strengthened himself in the Lord his God."

When you read the last part of the sixth verse in the King James version, it says, *"...but David encouraged himself in the Lord his God."*

Here is what happened. David's life was in danger because King Saul was a threat to him.

To be faced with as many disappointments as David faced would cause some to give up in despair or become addicted to their trials. Don't waste your sorrows on unnecessary things. Learn to encourage yourself. Discouragement is a strong demonic force.

When David killed Goliath, Saul seeing David returning from the battlefront, sought to benefit from his sudden popularity. He calls for David and begins to inquire as to who he was and what his future plans were. He was calculating how he might further his own agenda from a relationship with this newly discovered hero. With a few of his men and his son Jonathan by his side, Saul began to craftily bait the shepherd boy. David wasn't nearly as naïve as Saul was hoping he will be.

As David began to speak, it became clear that Saul had underestimated him, but Jonathan was captivated by David's words, after all he had lived for years under the control and ambitious dictatorship of his father. The question that turned the direction of David's life was the answer that likewise turned Jonathan's heart. And Saul said to him,

"Whose son are you, young man? "So, David answered, "I am the son of your servant Jesse the Bethlehemite" (1 Samuel 17:58).

This question steered the destinies of David and Jonathan into a new path. As David described his father, Jesse, Jonathan knew that the young shepherd had something in his father that the young prince had never experienced. Saul may have produced the natural seed that brought Jonathan into being, but Saul had fallen far short of being a father. Listening to David talk, Jonathan realised it took more than procreation to make a man a father. That same day Saul insisted that David stay in the palace and go no more home to his father.

I believe that God is still today connecting people for His purposes. God may join us together with people who were raised in the house of Saul, our associations sometimes will be with people delivered straight out of deep sin. The Hebrew word that describes what happened when the soul of Jonathan was 'knit' with David is *qashar* and it means 'to tie, to physically confine or compact together in a league of love; to knit stronger together,' and it is used only this one time in the Bible. It says in 1 Samuel 18:4

> *"And Jonathan took off the robe that was on him and gave it to David, with his armour, even to his sword and his bow and his belt."*

Jonathan's robe placed him next in line to be king. Yet, David had been anointed in a private ceremony by Prophet Samuel to be the monarch because God had already rejected Saul. Saul had no idea that God had already picked his replacement, and that the replacement was now living under his roof. This is powerful what was happing here. Jonathan was giving up his right to the throne to David!

David behaved himself wisely while serving Saul, he became accepted in the sight of all the men of war and all the people, not to mention Saul's own servants. He was set over the armies of war.

Soon jealousy set in. As careful as David was to never draw attention to himself, it seemed the people always venerated him. There was a parade for Saul to celebrate the victory over Goliath. That occasion was to honour Saul, but the women paraded into the streets singing and dancing together exclaiming,

> *"Saul has slain his thousands, And David his ten thousands"* (1 Samuel 18:7b).

This gesture was the last straw that broke the camel's back. Read on in verses 8 and 9,

"Then Saul was very angry, and the saying displeased him; and he said, "They have ascribed to David ten thousands, and to me they have ascribed only thousands. Now what more can he have but the kingdom?" So Saul eyed David from that day forward."

Saul became obsessed with destroying David even though he continued to serve Saul faithfully. He tried twice to kill David with a javelin, David escaped out his hand two times, yet he never allowed bitterness to take root in his spirit.

Finally, David ran away from Saul and joined up with their enemies and lived there.

"And David said in his heart, "Now I shall perish someday by the hand of Saul. There is nothing better for me than that I should speedily escape to the land of the Philistines; and Saul will despair of me, to seek me anymore in any part of Israel. So, I shall escape out of his hand." Then David arose and went over with the six hundred men who were with him to Achish the son of Maoch, king of Gath. So, David dwelt with Achish at Gath, he and his men, each man with his household, and David with his two wives, Ahinoam the Jezreelitess, and Abigail the Carmelitess, Nabal's widow. And it was told Saul that David had fled to Gath; so, he sought him no more." (1 Samuel 27:1-4).

From here he went out against his own people and battled against them and killed them on behalf of Achish, the Philistine King. It seems he had it nice, his army of former outcasts has proven to be quite a force to be reckoned with. David, who had fought on the side of the Philistines was getting ready with his 600 men to fight with the Philistines against his own people, but the other Philistine commanders and kings became suspicious of him and asked king Achish of Gath to send him back.

It was a three-day trip and as they went, David and his men no doubt talked excitedly about how good it would feel to get home to their families, to enjoy the embrace of their wives and children, to eat a good home cooked meal and to sleep in their own beds. But as they came over the hill and looked down on what they expected to be a peaceful domestic scene, they were horrified to see nothing but a pile of smouldering ashes! Their town was burned to the ground, their families were nowhere in sight, and everything they owned was gone.

Fear grips their hearts as they discover what could only be described as nightmare. In their absence, the Amalekites invaded their city, burned it with fire, and took their wives and children captive. They took captive the women, and all who were in it, both young and old but they did not kill any of them. They had Abigail among the captives. A woman with good judgment, intelligence and prayerful. With God no experience is wasted.

Abigail in 1 Samuel chapter 25 was used by God to stop David from destroying her household, when Nabal treated David with contempt. I believe with the grace of God upon her life, she managed to convince the Amalekites to spare the captives. Even before the Amalekites attacked, she must have encouraged the other women to intercede for their husbands who had gone to war and for their children. Their safety was no coincidence. Your prayers are not in vain! They provide covering for your life, family and others. Don't give up praying for your families and communities, your prayers attract God's protection over you in the day of trouble.

"Then David and the people who were with him lifted up their voices and wept, until they had no more power to weep." (1 Samuel 30:4).

You may have seasons of weeping even as a believer in Christ. Tears are prayers too. Your situation has made you cry until you can cry no more.

"So, David and his men came to the city, and behold, it was burned with fire; and their wives, and their sons, and their daughters, were taken captives. Then David and the people that were with him lifted up their voice and wept, until they had no more power to weep". (I Sam 30:3-4)

The Lord will wipe those tears. He will show you His compassion. He will turn your sorrow into joy. Psalm 30:5 says,

"Weeping endures a night, but joy comes in the morning".

I remember a few others whose tears attracted God. Hagar and her son Ishmael cried, and God heard, and an angel was sent to encourage her, and God showed her water (Gen 21:16-19). Hannah too cried and God answered her prayer. Hezekiah also had tears. 2 Kings 20:5 says,

"I have heard your prayer; I have seen your tears."

I hear the Lord say to you, "don't be discouraged for I am with you. You will rise again. You will recover all you have lost. For nothing is lost, I have preserved it for you. Your prayers provided a covering for your family, your dreams, and your possession. I the Lord your God will fight for you and will recover it all." But like David you must rise above your discouragement. The Lord not only hears our prayers, but He also sees our tears!

David and his men were bitter and discouraged because the Amalekites had destroyed their city Ziklag and taken their families captive, but just when David thinks it cannot get any worse, it does. They turned against David.

"Now David was greatly distressed, for the people spoke of stoning him, because the soul of all the people was grieved, every man for his sons and his daughters. But David strengthened himself in the Lord his God." Vs 6.

When we are faced with challenges, do we plan a rescue, or do we look for someone to blame?

Situations sometimes could take a different shape when you are made to believe that you are reaping the consequences of your calamities, that you are responsible for the mess you are in. This could be the worst form of despair. Add to that the accusations of those you thought were your friends, who now are blaming you for problems they're having because of their failure. You feel alone, rejected, and as if everything you've been working toward has gone up in smoke.

When this verse says that David "was greatly distressed", I believe it wasn't simply because of what the Amalekites had done, it was because his warriors turned against him. Six hundred men against one man! If you have been a leader, you will agree with me that leadership is a lonely place. We look after others, counsel them, and watch their backs when they are in need, but you go home alone on your own. I believe that leaders must always take time to look after themselves, they must seek to develop self-love and self-care. Don't neglect your own soul!

Let me share a few things with you which I believe David did to encourage himself in the Lord, which you can use today as tools of encouraging yourself.

When faced with discouragement, David prayed
"So, David inquired of the Lord, saying, "Shall I pursue this troop? Shall I overtake them? "And He answered him, "Pursue, for you shall surely overtake them and without fail recover all."
Vs 8.

He enquired of the Lord, he didn't just go, he asked God first. When I am low in spirit I like to pray and every time I do, I get strengthened. Isn't it funny that most times when faced with issues, what we do is to come up with our own schemes and formula and ask God to put his blessing on them? The moment we learn to ask His opinion on issues, that moment our victory begins. He asked the Lord, "Shall I pursue this band?" Many would not have bothered to ask the question: "These guys stole our families and our possessions. Let's go get 'em!" But David deliberately stopped to ask the Lord if he should pursue this band to try to recover what they had taken.

What if God had said, "No, David, your wives and your possessions are gone"? It would have been hard, but I think David would have submitted. You can't write your own terms when you come to the Lord. You can't say, "Lord, I'll come back if You will do what I want." He is the Lord, which means that He does what He wants, which doesn't always fit with what I want. Submission means that I let Him call the shots. Whether He says, "It's all gone," or whether He graciously gives it back, I submit.

Prayer is a powerful force! John Wesley once said, 'God does nothing except in response to believing prayer.' Believe me when I say it, prayer changes things. It builds confidence in us, which acts as a great encouragement.

David himself was a man of prayer as seen in the book of Psalms. He knew how to express his feelings before God.
But when David encouraged himself in the Lord he prayed with confidence and the wonderful promise came from the Lord:

"You shall surely pursue and overtake and by all means recover."

David would not have heard anything if he had chosen to remain discouraged.

The mountains that we are facing get weaker as we pray against them. So, it is dangerous to get discouraged because it could be when you are just about to have your breakthrough.

Release your situation into the hands of the Lord: The songwriter Charles Albert Tindley wrote, *"take your burden to the Lord and leave it there."* Refuse to doubt, refuse to waste your night working it out with your brain. Just leave them there!

"Casting all your care upon Him, for He cares for you." 1 Peter 5:7

It does not say cast some, but all. If you do not hand your cares over to Him, then don't blame Him if He does not work on them.

David encouraged himself through prayer to God. The life of David was a life of prayer. He cried out to God and each time he failed to do so, he often got into trouble. He was the Psalmist who was always in prayer or praising God for His goodness.

"I prayed to the Lord, and he answered me. He freed me from all my fears." Psalm 34:4 (NLT).

God does not want you to live in fear. He will hear your cries. He will deliver you from your fears. Pray to our Heavenly Father, and you will be greatly encouraged.

When faced with discouragement, David made great declarations

He made declarations of God's ability to protect him from his enemies. He also declared who God was to him. He told the problems how big his God was. Psalm number 27 is a good example.

"The Lord is my light and my salvation; Whom shall I fear?
The Lord is the strength of my life; Of whom shall I be afraid?
² When the wicked came against me to eat up my flesh, my enemies
and foes, they stumbled and fell. ³ Though an army may encamp
against me, my heart shall not fear; Though war may rise against
me, in this I will be confident."
In verse 13 David said, *"I would have lost heart, unless I had*
believed That I would see the goodness of the Lord In the land of
the living."

Job also did the same in Job 19:25. After narrating how badly people were treating him because of what he was going through, he declared,

"For I know that my Redeemer lives, And He shall stand at last
on the earth."

Encourage yourself through praise and songs

David called for Abiathar the priest to bring him the linen ephod. He learned that the power of praise would turn his captivity. He put on the ephod, the garment of praise for his spirit of heaviness (see Isaiah 61:3). He was about to praise his way out of discouragement. There are times when no one will encourage you, so you must learn to encourage yourself in the Lord through singing.

David was a musician. When Saul was tormented by an evil spirit, they called for David to sing and the spirit left Saul (1 Sam16:14-23, 2 Sam 22). David worshiped and praised his way out of despair. His men were no help, held fast in the clutches of helpless depression. David was encouraged by the power of praise. Many times, in his life, David responds to difficult situations by singing. He creates a new song. He worships. Just like Paul and Silas in prison in the book of Acts. They were going about their daily ministry doing what the Lord had called to do in Philippi, after he saw the vision of a man who said, "Come over to Macedonia and help us!" They went. The Lord used them mightily and Lydia and her entire household believed and were baptised. She convinced them into spending a few days in her home. It was while here that they started a daily prayer journey and on one of those prayer trips they met a girl who was possessed by a spirit of divination, she earned a lot of money for her masters by telling fortunes. Paul got so exasperated by her constant interruptions and cast the spirit out of her and they were thrown in prison. What did Paul and Silas do? Around midnight Paul and Silas were praying and singing hymns to God, and the other prisoners were listening. They sang! And you remember what happened next. At the 'midnight hour' of your life what do you do? Complain? Ring 911? Curse and swear? Let us learn to sing during our difficult and discouraging times and see God bring mighty encouragement to us.

We can all testify that some songs are anointed and can release the power of God to change situations. Let me say this to you, when discouraged, sing! and if you can't sing, listen to uplifting gospel music. I have learnt the power of listening to what I call 'soaking music', they have been a source of great encouragement. And if you can dance, by all means dance! Oh, how I love those times in our African churches! if you can do this, trust me, discouragement will flee. Put on your garment of praise.

David encouraged himself with past victories

When David left Jonathan emptyhanded, he first ran to Ahimelech the priest for food and hopefully a weapon. When he arrived, there was no food, only the hallowed communion bread (see 1 Samuel 21:1-6). He asked for five loaves of bread and received communion instead. There is a great assistance that comes from communion with God and His saints.

When David asked for weapons, Ahimelech was confused that the man after God's heart is suddenly depending on carnal weapons. When in fear most often we are tempted to go back to comfort zones of the flesh. Perhaps we should remind ourselves that

'the weapons of our warfare are not carnal, but mighty through God to the pulling down of strong holds' 2 Corinthians 10:4.

The only weapon David received was the past weapon he has already taken from the Philistine champion. Your current situation is not going to be solved in the future. It has already been solved in your past.

"So, the priest said, "The sword of Goliath the Philistine, whom you killed in the Valley of Elah, there it is, wrapped in a cloth behind the ephod. If you will take that, take it. For there is no other except that one here. And David said, "There is none like it; give it to me."" 1 Samuel 21:9.

This is called testimony. It has power to encourage both the testifier and listeners.

David said in Psalm 34:1-3

"I will bless the Lord at all times; His praise shall continually be in my mouth. My soul shall make its boast in the Lord; The humble shall hear of it and be glad. Oh, magnify the Lord with me, and let us exalt His name together."

Even when he was ridiculed by Goliath, he remembered how God had helped him tear the lion and the bear that had come after the sheep he was taking care of (1 Sam 17:34-36). Encourage yourself by reminding yourself of the good things God did for you or for others. Perhaps He had answered some prayers before? Thank Him for those things. You can also get encouragement from other people's testimonies. The bible is full of the great things God did for people and he is no respecter of persons. He will do it for you too.

Here's what he had said to Goliath so many years before.

"Today the Lord will conquer you, and I will kill you and cut off your head. And then I will give the dead bodies of your men to the birds and wild animals, and the whole world will know that there is a God in Israel! 47 And everyone assembled here will know that the Lord rescues his people, but not with sword and spear. This is the Lord's battle, and he will give you to us!" 48 As Goliath moved closer to attack, David quickly ran out to meet him." 1 Samuel 17:46-48 (NLT)

When David remembered the Lord, he was absolutely fearless. He said,

"The Lord is my light and my salvation whom shall I fear? The Lord is the stronghold of my life of whom shall I be afraid?"
Psalm 27:1 (NIV).

"If God be for us, who can be against us?" Romans 8:31

David encouraged himself by remembering God's past deliverances. When you feel distressed and discouraged, remember how many times that God had delivered you, and you will be encouraged.

He asked for help

David called for Abiathar the priest, Ahimelech's son, to bring him the linen ephod. It was Abiathar who had run into the camp when David was distressed and surrounded by hurting people after Saul decreed to have him killed. He surrounded himself with people who knew God.
In verse 7,

"Then David said to Abiathar the priest, Ahimelech's son, "Please bring the ephod here to me." And Abiathar brought the ephod to David."

When Jesus asked Peter to come to him walking on water, he got out and started walking to the Master. He was walking on water! But then he began to look upon the waves and probably asking himself what was happening, so he began to sink and when Peter began to sink, he asked for help.

"And Peter answered Him and said, "Lord, if it is You, command me to come to You on the water." So He said, "Come." And when Peter had come down out of the boat, he walked on the water to go to Jesus. But when he saw that the wind was boisterous, he was afraid; and beginning to sink he cried out, saying, "Lord, save me!""

It is very important that we look for spiritual leaders to mentor and help us when we need them. Some people may have been swept over today and some even die, not because they don't have people who love them but because they wouldn't talk to anyone. Every problem has a solution and someone who has seen worse than you. There are people who are trained in other areas where we might be needing help. There are spiritual counsellors or mental health experts who can help us when we need these kinds of help. You will be helping yourself if you learn to seek for help. I think most people refuse to ask for help because of pride or even because of shame.

During our Bible study in church the other day, I was sharing how it is that many religious leaders have misled others into thinking that when you are a Christian, then you are beyond the help of others. A pastor who preaches that a Christian is not supposed to be sick, or who paints a false picture of a 'marriage-made-in-heaven' only causes others to believe that they are lesser Christians. And when these Christians fall sick or meet some personal discouragement, they fear to ask for help because of shame. Something must be wrong with me; they must be saying to themselves. No! Please go ahead and ask for help.

*"No temptation has overtaken you except such as is common to man; but God is faithful, who will not allow you to be tempted beyond what you are able, but with the temptation will also make the way of escape, that you may be able to bear it."*1 Corinthians 10:13

Even as David asked for help from his trusted friends and from his God, so, everyone today who asks God for divine intervention will be saved. No matter who you are and what you have done, the merciful God will reach out to you and pull you up.

"Scripture reassures us, "No one who trusts God like this—heart and soul—will ever regret it." It's exactly the same no matter what a person's religious background may be: the same God for all of us, acting the same incredibly generous way to everyone who calls out for help. "Everyone who calls, 'Help, God!' gets help." Romans 10:11-13(MSG).

It is as simple as that. Everyone who calls out, 'help, God!' will get help. Are you in need of divine help, just stop right here, and yell out with all your heart to Him, 'help, God!'

Rise up in power and do spiritual warfare
In verse 10 is says,
"But David pursued, he and four hundred men; for two hundred stayed behind, who were so weary that they could not cross the Brook Besor."

When faced with discouraging and challenging situations, don't just cry and cry. Some situations call for spiritual warfare and you will need to take up your position against the enemy whose mission is to kill, steal and destroy. (Jn 10:10).

You can do something about your situation and with God's blessing you will succeed.

Rise up in the power and authority that Jesus has given you and go after what is yours.

Imagine what would have happened if David and his men had sat back and not gone to rescue their wives and children?

Jesus says that all things are possible to him that believes. Perhaps you have problems that seem to defy solution. You have come to your wits end. Hear this, all things are possible to him that believes.

The Bible does not say that all things are possible to him that worries. When we say things are impossible, it means that we have arrived at self-defeat. Whatever the situation may be, believe that all things are possible. So, see that possibility and you will see what the Lord will do.

God told David that he would recover everything, and David took God at His word. He believed God and acted upon that belief in pursuing this band and fighting to take back what had been lost. It would not have done for David to sit around the ruins of Ziklag saying, "I'm just trusting the Lord." He had to go and fight to recover what had been stolen.

Genuine faith is always active and obedient. Faith doesn't passively sit around saying, "I believe." Faith is taking God at His Word, often in the face of overwhelming circumstances to the contrary. It involves acting obediently upon that Word until what is promised becomes reality.

He left some people behind

Vs 9 *"So David went, he and the six hundred men who were with him, and came to the Brook Besor, where those stayed who were left behind."*

To move on in life and onto serious encouragement, you don't need everyone around you. Some people might need to go! Being able to break away from toxic people can make a great difference in your life. Allow only positive people who are sincere about who you are, but I don't mean you should surround yourself with only 'yes' men. If you have only these 'yes' people around, then you will never get sincere encouragement. True friends will criticise you constructively and with love.

"but, speaking the truth in love, may grow up in all things into Him who is the head—Christ." Ephesians 4:15

When you get criticised by those who know you well and who love you, it is easier for you to accept this because they know what you are capable of. You are convinced that they are transparent about their judgement. Let your company be people who enrich and empower you, people who enable you to transcend yourself and grow. This sort of support group can strengthen you in moments of weakness and bring you up when you are down. They form the backbone for your progress in life. Allow only people who share your vision and who are willing to support you in pursuing that vision. Run away from relationships that are not mutually constructive, that seek to bring you down rather than challenge and elevate you.

Although it hurts when criticised by friends, I do have some trusted critics. These are people who tell me the things I need to hear, not necessary what I want to hear. I trust their judgement; I trust their vision of me. They challenge me and make me stretch mentally and intellectually, personally, and spiritually. I get feedback from them that I would not get anywhere else and even though it doesn't always feel good to hear the criticism and challenges, I know they care about me and about my growth. So, I listen and learn. I suspect you are like me too.

My wife is my best friend and knows me better than any other person. At the dark and in daylight she tells me what no one else will say and I am forever grateful for her.

We have to be willing to seek out those with wisdom and say, 'I don't know what to do; help me.' *"All of us are like the blind man at some point in our lives, standing on the corner, waiting for someone to lead us across."*- Joe Frazier

You are not joined at the hip with your friends. Be prepared to acknowledge when a relationship has soured and go your separate ways. It doesn't have to be an angry parting. You may need to say, 'look here we are growing in different directions, our values have changed, our goals and objectives are different now, maybe we need to shake hands and say goodbye.'

I strongly believe that some encouragement can come by letting some unhelpful people out of your life.

When God told David to go after the Amalekites and recover what they stole, he needed to go with only people who were ready and who were of the same mind and purpose. Some of the warriors just needed to be left behind. Two hundred men stayed put at the Brook Besor, they were so weary that they couldn't cross the brook, but I have a feeling that most of them may have pretended to be weak because they didn't share in the same passion and drive as David did. They might have asked themselves, 'what's the point chasing after what was already gone? Let us just resign to fate.' This is what I am saying, there are people who don't just agree with your visions and dreams, they are miles away from what you believe, it might worth it to ask yourself if you need these people in your life as you make your journey of destiny.

We must develop self-love

Self-love allows you to embrace who you are and, as a result, become better at loving not only yourself but others.

"The second is this: 'You shall love your neighbour as yourself.' There is no other commandment greater than these."
Mark 12:31

Earlier on, I told you that leadership sometimes could be a lonely place. If you are a leader, I would advise that you take time to strengthen and encourage yourself, because, if you neglect your own soul, you will die untimely and you know what? The work will continue!

Each one of us, no matter our role should develop self-care and self-love, especially when you are faced with difficult and discouraging situations which seem to hit you from within. David was hit so hard, not only because of the calamity that befell Ziklag, but very hard from the action of his men.
Self-love is an intentional journey.

"But David ..." This is one of the many great "buts" in the Bible. Everything around David was gloom and doom. His property was either destroyed or stolen. His wives were gone, and he didn't know at this point if he would ever see them again. His men were talking of killing him. "But David!" He intentionally, deliberately rejected the faithless gloom and doom of his men. He intentionally looked beyond the smouldering ruins of Ziklag to the greatness of his God.

David's strong intention is also seen in the Hebrew verb, "strengthened himself." It implies persistent and continuous effort. There is nothing passive about coming back to the Lord at a time of despair. It doesn't happen accidentally. Sometimes, like the psalmist, you have to grab yourself by the lapels and talk to yourself:

"Why are you in despair, O my soul? And why have you become disturbed within me? Hope in God, for I shall again praise Him, the help of my countenance, and my God" (43:5; see 42:5, 11).

Like the prodigal son, you must determine, "I will get up out of this pigsty and go back to my father!" The way back is always intentional.

Personally, sometimes I do crazy things like looking myself in the mirror inside my bathroom and speaking words of faith to the guy behind the mirror!

See divine possibilities

See that the blessings you need can come. You must see that every problem has an end and that the end of a trial will come. Begin to see that God can do something in your life, that the pain, the fear and the financial problem can come to an end. Begin to see the possibility that life is turning for the better and things would begin to happen. In the Bible, those who reclaimed their safe spaces did so because they saw that it was possible. They pursued it seriously, they did not give up, they kept going and going until what they wanted came into their hands. What I mean is that if you don't see it, you won't have the audacity to pursue change, you have to have a mental picture of your victory first, at least you could say, I tried.

David encouraged himself by knowing God was in control of his life. Are you a child of God? Believe me, God is in control of your life, not the devil, or your government.

"My times are in your hands; deliver me from the hands of my enemies, from those who pursue me." Psalm 31:5

David prayed for deliverance but at the same time knew that his "times are in God's hand."

Look at the woman with the issue of blood. Before she left her home, she had it settled: "I know that all I need to do is to touch the helm of His garment and I shall be made whole. I don't even want the man to pray for me. It is not necessary." She had already seen the possibility. The woman saw the possibility and that was it.

Jacob too saw the possibility and stood there until he got it (Genesis 32:26). Blind Bartimaeus saw the possibility (Mark 10:46-52). The Syrophoenician woman asked Jesus to heal her daughter and Jesus said,

"No, I cannot take the food of the children and give it to dogs."

The woman was not discouraged. She was not upset. She was determined to get what she wanted. She stayed there until the Saviour had to answer her prayer (Mark 7:24-29). None of us was born to be in a dark situation forever. Change comes to those who see possibilities. When you don't see divine possibilities, you settle for anything in life and you will be a person without a bright future, and anyone without a bright future will always settle for the average life.

The best thing to do when faced with any discouraging situation would be to encourage yourself. Together with all I have said, I believe we could encourage ourselves also through fellowship. I've reminded you of the Bible verse *'iron sharpens iron'*, and now I want you to remember what the writer of Hebrews says

"This is not the time to pull away and neglect meeting together, as some have formed the habit of doing. In fact, we should come together even more frequently, eager to encourage and urge each other onward as we anticipate that day dawning." Hebrews 10:25(TPT).

A time of discouragement is never the time to pull away from others, it is a natural thing to do but we should try to avoid this. It says we should even come together more frequently. We could 'meet' either in person or on-line, but from experience we have known that online fellowships and hybrid church becomes more relaxed and enjoyable when we have known our 'members' in person prior to online meetings. Leading online events and hybrid church is one skill that I have acquired and grown in during the past few months, but I am sure when I say that the result is better when you meet in person, and for some people, the first contact would be online and then this will lead to a time of in-person catchup.

Great encouragement comes also through reading of good books and listening to inspirational speakers. This is something I do always. I've been told that great leaders are good readers. This is a habit I have carried with me since I was a little boy growing up in a rural village in Africa. I would read every piece of paper on my way on errands meandering through the long narrow bush paths and stopping on the way to read through every paper poster on the wall. When I talk about listening to speakers, I need to drop a caveat right here to say that there are many things all over the internet today that are utterly useless.

Social media has provided the platform for people to post any irrelevant and time-wasting material, don't waste your time listening to everything and reading any and everything you see, some things are clearly misleading, even some hard copy materials. I know we should censor what our kids read and watch these days, and Anita and I have been very good at this. We encourage our children to read and to develop themselves both by reading hard copies and soft copies, but we guide them through it all. I believe adults should also put on some sort of checks because, like or not, what you watch will surely affect you.

Chapter Two
Finding Joy Amidst Fearful Circumstances

Life is too sacred to be wasted in fear. We are told that the average life span is 80. And most people begin their working life at 18 and retire at 67. So, we spend pretty much all our life working. You don't want to while away your life for nothing, do you? There is no second attempt at life. It has been proven that joy increases our intelligence, productivity, and our creativity. Joy makes people live longer! Go and check the life of optimists, they live longer than pessimists.

When you discover joy for yourself, you have indeed received great delight and a gladness of heart because the word joy in the Greek is *'chara'* which means 'gladness and delight.' I make bold to say that joy is not circumstantial, it is not superficial, unlike happiness. The world today is in a rat race for happiness. Will this person or this thing make me happy? Will I derive pleasure from this? These are what we hear people say. Happiness is what people seek after; it is elusive though. It exists merely on the soul level. Joy is not something we seek, but an experience that comes from the spirit.

The absence of joy isn't sorrow. Sorrow could be a normal reaction to loss, disappointment, or difficult situations, which we all could have. Feeling sad is just another part of being human, but these usually go away after some time, and you go on with your life. But when a person doesn't have joy, they are indeed hopeless. They will need divine help. I want you to know that if you are without Christ, you are already in a hopeless situation and fear can rule your life.

You know that many things can weigh you down even as a redeemed person. Sicknesses and disease, daily stresses of life, the ups and downs of family, the wear and tear of marriage, parenting and even a little thing as traffic. Don't let them steal you joy.

Joy is supernatural. It flows from a quiet confidence of a genuine relationship with God and His son Jesus Christ.

"Every good gift and every perfect gift is from above, and comes down from the Father of lights, with whom there is no variation or shadow of turning." James 1:17

The experience of real joy is imparted to the saints of God from the Spirit into their innermost being – the spirit man. You can find this experience useful even amid fearful circumstance.

"Now may the God of hope fill you with all joy and peace in believing, that you may abound in hope by the power of the Holy Spirit." Romans 15:13

Joy flows out of an attitude of gratitude. You will believe with me that not every day is a good day. So, when you have joy, this doesn't mean you might not be depressed sometimes. We see in the Bible that our Lord and Saviour Jesus Christ had a feeling a feeling of depression.

"He went a little farther and fell on His face, and prayed, saying, "O My Father, if it is possible, let this cup pass from Me; nevertheless, not as I will, but as You will." Matthew 26:39

We also see throughout scripture that men and women of God were depressed, both in the old and the new testaments. A good example is Job. Hannah also was depressed by what her rival did to her (1 Samuel). The powerful prophet Elijah was greatly depressed and even had some suicidal thoughts. The apostle Paul went through some very low moments in his life journey. We might have some days of 'spiritual low percentage' but still are filled with deep inner joy. I'm not expecting you to go around 'high-fiving' everyone you meet on the way simply because you are a child of God. We are not called to be a 'happy-clappy' bunch of people, but what I would like to see is that we are always a 'glass-half-full' kind of people. The danger of not being full of joy is that things could begin to dry up and everything in life becomes ordinary daily chores and when someone gets to this stage, they will want to withdraw from others and even from life in total. We are commanded to be full of joy just like we've been commanded by the Bible to love with Agape kind of love.

As you cling tight to Jesus Christ and abide daily in your saving relationship with Him, you will begin to have the fulness of Joy.

"You will show me the path of life; In Your presence is fullness of joy; At Your right hand are pleasures forevermore." Psalm 16:11

When a believer walks very closely with the Holy Spirit, He releases joy into their system, this keeps it running through them on a very regular and consistent basis.

I have a feeling that you might be asking to know how you could have joy and let it grow. First and foremost, this is possible through the Word of God. A time came in the life of the prophet Jeremiah that he was so depressed that he decided to do something that we all can do.

"Your words were found, and I ate them, And Your word was to me the joy and rejoicing of my heart; For I am called by Your name, O Lord God of hosts." Jeremiah 15:16

When you engage with the Bible, don't just read it, 'eat' it. That means we should meditate and reflect on God's Word. One of my favourite passages of scripture is Isaiah 26:3
"You will keep him in perfect peace, whose mind is stayed on You, because he trusts in You."
And when you fill your heart with God's Word, decide to obey them. We are mostly full of joy when we know that we do the right things.

You must also learn to fill your space with positive sound. Listen to good worship songs and expose yourself to positive things. There is too much garbage thrown at us today from the media. If you really want to live a positive life, you must put the phone and the computer away! Trust me, this thing is killing this generation. Technology is good, I must say that, but we have to guard against the obsession that can go with them.
In Philippians 4: 4, we find a detail for joy, which we find difficult in our society today.

Philippians 4:4: *"Rejoice in the Lord always. Again, I will say, rejoice!"*

Joy is an expensive commodity, an expensive commodity which we can easily slip through if we don't take care of. Joy is not just a decision or an "always happy face."
There is much more to joy than just being superficially happy. "To be joyous" means to have deep inner contentment, balance, and happiness.

This joy does not depend on the circumstances of life. Whoever is happy in the Lord knows that God has everything under control and therefore feels an exceptional security. The joy we have in the Lord is our strength or our protection.

"Then he said to them, "Go your way, eat the fat, drink the sweet, and send portions to those for whom nothing is prepared; for this day is holy to our Lord. Do not sorrow, for the joy of the LORD is your strength. "Nehemiah 8:10

It is the joy of the Lord, not the joy of the country you reside in or the city you come from. The joy of the Lord is your strength. After hearing the words of the law, the people began to cry. They recognized that they were guilty and must fear the penalties threatened in the law. Ezra's words of encouragement are not intended to distract from this but rather to make it clear that the ultimate goal of the law is not sadness but joy.

Real joy is protection from bitterness, protection from being crushed by worry. Those who rejoice in the Lord are not worried or desperate but accept God's plan for their life and claim God's promises for themselves. If we love God and do His will, He will direct all experiences in our lives so that they work for our good.

"And we know that all things work together for good to those who love God, to those who are the called according to His purpose."
Romans 8:28

Joy is, among other things, a decision. Real joy is only possible through God's grace. Joy is related to the word for grace in ancient Greek, meaning that real joy can only be obtained in connection with and dependent on God's grace. Those who trust God completely and accept God's plan for their life will enjoy the constant joy because they know where what they are experiencing comes from.

Paul uses the word joy very often in Philippians, even though he was imprisoned and could have received the death penalty. He did not complain, was not disappointed, did not speak negatively, but had accepted God's plan for his life. This attitude is also a gift from God.
Joy is also a fruit of the Spirit.

> *"But the fruit of the Spirit is love, joy, peace, longsuffering, kindness, goodness, faithfulness,"* Galatians 5:22

Biblical joy, or the joy of the Lord, is not just outward, nor does it depend on our circumstances, mood, or feelings. If we walk in the Spirit, that is, place ourselves under His guidance and live by His power, we will have joy as part of the fruit of the Spirit. The fruit is brought about by God and is not something we deserve or can do ourselves.

> *"These things I have spoken to you, that My joy may remain in you, and that your joy may be full."* John 15:11

Believing in the Lord means being in connection with Jesus Christ. So, deep joy only arises in connection with Jesus Christ. It describes a close relationship and fellowship with Jesus Christ, as shown in the picture "... vine and branch" (John 15: 5).

All human beings are born with a sinful nature and are therefore dead (separated from God) until they believe in Jesus Christ to become saved. So, the basis of joy in the life of a Christian is what Jesus Christ did for them on the cross and what He does for us every day.

"Therefore, if anyone is in Christ, he is a new creation; old things have passed away; behold, all things have become new." 2 Corinthians 5:17

Jesus made a new person out of you and me; this is enough for you to rejoice. The reverse is also true; Joy is not possible when we sin. When you put yourself in a conscious and deliberate sin, this then will interfere with your communion with the Lord and by extension, the joy of the Lord in you.

"If we say that we have fellowship with Him, and walk in darkness, we lie and do not practice the truth." 1 John 1:6

But the amazing thing about Jesus is that we are allowed to come to Him again and again and confess our sins, and thus our joy is renewed and strengthened again and again. In Philippians 4:4, the "rejoice" is in the present tense, i.e., in the present, which means rejoice continually. Because of the connection we have with Jesus Christ and our faith in Him, it is possible always to rejoice. This is emphasized by the word "always" (without interruption). It is possible to rejoice always because God has made many promises and is faithful to keep His word. For example:

"The LORD is my shepherd; I shall not want." Psalm 23:1

Because the Good Shepherd guides and cares for us regularly, we can rejoice instead of worry. If your relationship with our Lord is in order, you will always be able to rejoice.

"These things I have spoken to you, that My joy may remain in you, and that your joy may be full." John 15:11
Jesus makes our joy complete.

Here are some benefits of joy:

Beauty

God gives you a unique beauty when you decide to be joyous. Joy is the best beauty treatment that anyone can discover.

> *"A merry heart makes a cheerful countenance, but by sorrow of the heart the spirit is broken."* Proverbs 15:13

but in another bible version, it says

> *"A joyful heart beautifies the face…"*

Health

If you suffer from any disease, mainly in your bones, you could start by deciding to cast out the sadness to make your healing effective.

> *"A merry heart does good, like medicine, but a broken spirit dries the bones."* Proverbs 17:22

Fortress

A new force comes into your being when you choose to be content. Do not get depressed, or discouraged, because that weakens you. Activate the joy that God has given you.

> *"…Do not sorrow, for the joy of the LORD is your strength.""*
> Nehemiah 8:10b

Freedom

"But at midnight Paul and Silas were praying and singing hymns to God, and the prisoners were listening to them. Suddenly there was a great earthquake, so that the foundations of the prison were shaken; and immediately all the doors were opened, and everyone's chains were loosed." Acts 16: 25-26

We can experience this kind of freedom which Paul and Silas had that night. Let us decide to rejoice in praising God, and all the bonds of fear, depression, or whatever that is keeping us bound will be broken in Jesus name!

Hope

When you allow God to fill you with joy, you have great, steadfast hope. Cheer up, my friend, so you don't lose hope. Allow God's Joy to flow through you to be firm in waiting for his promises.

"Now may the God of hope fill you with all joy and peace in believing, that you may abound in hope by the power of the Holy Spirit." Romans 15:13

Chapter Three
Powerful Confessions in Dark Times

God created the world to be controlled physically by some natural laws and principles: and spiritually by supernatural laws and principles. He then made man in His own image and after His likeness as lord, king, and master to have dominion and rule over everything He created both in the physical and spiritual dimensions. He also set an example of His nature by speaking into existence the desire of His heart.
Learning to speak God's Word is one of the most important things that can ever happen to you.

What do I mean by confession? I am not talking about Religious Absolution, the thing we do to a religious figure to receive 'priestly pardon'. I am also not talking about your formal statement of admitting that you are guilty of a crime or your acknowledgement that you have done something about which you are ashamed or embarrassed. My idea is to define confession as 'to say the same things as God says.'

"Let your conduct be without covetousness; be content with such things as you have. For He Himself has said, "I will never leave you nor forsake you." So, we may boldly say: "The Lord is my helper; I will not fear. What can man do to me?" Hebrews 13:5,6

Darkness is the absence of light and illumination. Anyone of us can face periods of 'darkness', these could be times of personal troubles or global pandemic, they could be times of lack, sickness or persecution. It could be times of extreme hardship or discouragement. Days that are devoid of brightness. Genuinely, there are times when things don't go our way and during these moments it is quite natural to doubt what you believe. I want you to know however, that there are things which the enemy brings, coming from evil agents and forces and there are yet other things that life simply brings our way, whichever they are, we must learn to confess the powerful word of God over our life and situation.

Ladies and gentlemen, we live in a very dark world. The current state of our planet calls for serious and urgent action. Wickedness is on the increase and men and women are turning against what we have known as the foundations of good judgment and fairness. The Church, the body of Christ is fast being challenged by powers from hell and we see holiness and the evangelical faith under serious attack especially in the developed world. Like it or not, the Word of the Lord does not change. We live in a changing world, but the truth is timeless and unchanging. The Bible is still the inspired inerrant Word of God and holds supreme authority for faith and practice.

People of God must stand with the Word of the living God no matter where we live and no matter our generation. The Church, the body of Christ has always been counter cultural. We are not ruled by the customs and traditions of men but by the eternal Word of the everlasting God. He rules over the affairs of men, and if you remain faithful, your lifestyles and values are going to be at daggers drawn with the system of the world for the rest of your life, that is, if you decide to remain true to the kingdom of God and His Word.

You must choose to speak God's word in the middle of dark times, because your talk during hard times reveals your true strength. Our words do matter. Look not on the dark times but on God's words and His promised deliverance.
Our situations could work for us.

"For our light affliction, which is but for a moment, is working for us a far more exceeding and eternal weight of glory, while we do not look at the things which are seen, but at the things which are not seen. For the things which are seen are temporary, but the things which are not seen are eternal." 2 Corinthians 4:17,18

Go with the truth of God's word no matter your circumstances.

Once, during the last days of His earthly ministry, Jesus taught His disciples about the power in their confession. As they were traveling between Jerusalem and Bethany, Jesus was hungry but could not find any fruit on the fig, so He cursed the tree. The next day as they were coming out from the temple where Jesus had overturned the tables of the money changers and the seats of those who sold doves, Peter reminded him that the fig tree had died, Jesus didn't say anything in excitement rather He simply said,

"So Jesus answered and said to them, "Have faith in God. For assuredly, I say to you, whoever says to this mountain, 'Be removed and be cast into the sea,' and does not doubt in his heart, but believes that those things he says will be done, he will have whatever he says." Mark 11:22,23

This is a lesson to us about how to speak to our obstacles and mountains.

When Jesus said that you will *'have whatever he says,'* He says this in the present continuous tense. In the Greek language, this means 'you will keep having what you keep saying.' So, no matter what the circumstances are, let us keep saying what God says and pretty soon, we will have what we keep saying.

Never say what you don't want to see and don't you ever speak your fears, learn to speak words of faith.

When I was growing up in Nigeria, during farming seasons, my dad and all children engage actively in farming. We till the land, plant our seeds and crops, fertilize, and water them. Some people spray weed killers also. But if we skip a couple of weeks of watering, do you know what happens? The grass turns yellow; the weeds start growing, the crops start withering. Why? We have to keep doing this to get the result we desire for our crops.

As humans we have not exploited the fulness of the nature of God in our own life. Many times, we let negative words and thoughts pour out of us and affect our future. Errot Hatfield once said, *"3-inch tongue can bring down a 6-foot man."* However, the trend every heavenly conscious Christian must imbibe is powerful confessions even during dark moments. I have seen promising young people performing below their potential because they frustrated the outcome of their efforts with negative confessions even before a step of faith. I have heard people who prayed for powerful breakthroughs in anointing-filled events only to destroy their prayers with negative confessions immediately afterwards.

We have a duty to our generation to be who God has destined us to be; but we are faced with an enemy who knows how to cage our destinies by turning our greatest weapon – OUR THOUGHTS and TONGUES – against us.

The Bible says that God has elevated His word above all His names (see Psalm 138:2). The word is powerful, but it depends on the user. So many people today use the Word negatively, but when we move in powerful confessions, we find the miracle to getting what we need out of the Word. The word of God is quick and active; it is still relevant today to change our situations and circumstances.
That change will come through the word of God, rightly divided, and applied.

The scripture says,

"How forceful are right words! But what does your arguing prove?" Job 6:25

I want you to find out that there is power and a very active force that come from our words.

It is vital to every believer to understand the ability of words to shape our destiny and establish our future.

Jesus 'said' things into being, He didn't 'beg'

What we see throughout the Bible and indeed from the life and ministry of our Lord and Saviour Jesus Christ is that never did He 'beg' God for anything. He commanded things to happen and teaches us to do the same if we must see things turn around for our future and get answers to our prayers. He didn't sit around begging God the Father to do things.

As Christians (Christ-like people), we see from the Bible that we should confess God's word during difficult times. The problem with us sometimes is that we fail to command things according to God's will or we fail to align ourselves with God's will. Sin can also reduce a Christian to a beggar when they are supposed to be a 'commander'.

A time came in the life of prophet Ezekiel when he spoke the very words of God and commanded the bones, as he was instructed by God. I believe that if he had kept quiet or 'begged' the bones, the outcome would have been different.

"So, I prophesied as I was commanded; and as I prophesied, there was a noise, and suddenly a rattling; and the bones came together, bone to bone" (Ezekiel 37:7)

If a person isn't better informed through God's revealed word, they may pray something like, 'Oh God, please if it is your will, heal me, please'.
It is already His perfect will, people! He's basically waiting for you to speak it into existence. Didn't you read when Jesus said that healing is the bread of the believer?

"But He answered and said, "It is not good to take the children's bread and throw it to the little dogs" (Matthew 15:26)

Let's look at this scripture:

"A Gentile woman who lived there came to him, pleading, "Have mercy on me, O Lord, Son of David! For my daughter is possessed by a demon that torments her severely." But Jesus gave her no reply, not even a word. Then his disciples urged him to send her away. "Tell her to go away," they said. "She is bothering us with all her begging." Then Jesus said to the woman, "I was sent only to help God's lost sheep—the people of Israel." But she came and worshiped him, pleading again, "Lord, help me!" Jesus responded, "It isn't right to take food from the children and throw it to the dogs." She replied, "That's true, Lord, but even dogs are allowed to eat the scraps that fall beneath their masters' table." "Dear woman," Jesus said to her, "your faith is great. Your request is granted. "And her daughter was instantly healed." Matthew 15:22-28 (NLT)

When we learn to say things as commanded by God's word rather than begging things to come to pass, we will also have the mentality to keep at it. How do I mean, you may wonder? We speak God's revealed word and keep saying it. That's when the miracle is complete. Ezekiel was asked to command and speak to the dry bones, and from the outset God made it clear and gave a step-by-step process and outcome.

Breath → flesh →muscles →skin = life.

When he obeyed, there was a rattling noise and then bones came together to bones. They were covered with sinews and flesh and then human skin. At this point he didn't throw a party and pop some Champaign for achieving a level of success. I wonder if some people get stuck in-between miracles. I have always said that it is more difficult to handle success than it is failure. The Bible said at that point when it seemed Ezekiel had arrived, there was no breath.

" Indeed, as I looked, the sinews and the flesh came upon them, and the skin covered them over; but there was no breath in them"
(Ezekiel 37:8)

Had he stopped speaking when the bones received flesh, the miracle wouldn't have been sealed.

At other times in His earthly ministry, Jesus set examples for us. In Matthew 8, it says

"When He had come down from the mountain, great multitudes followed Him. ² And behold, a leper came and worshiped Him, saying, "Lord, if You are willing, You can make me clean." ³ Then Jesus put out His hand and touched him, saying, "I am willing; be cleansed. "Immediately his leprosy was cleansed."

Did you see that? Jesus commanded him to be healed, He didn't beg the sickness to go. "of course, it is my will", He answered to the man, so be healed! On another occasion, Jesus was living in Capernaum and teaching the people there, and one day the people gathered in such large numbers that there was no room left inside the house where He was teaching, not even outside the door. Some men came carrying a paralyzed man but could not get inside, so they made an opening in the roof above Jesus and then lowered the man down. When Jesus saw their faith, He said to the paralyzed man,

"Son, your sins are forgiven."

Some of the teachers of the law interpreted this as blasphemy since God alone can forgive sins. The gospel of Mark states that Jesus

"knew in His spirit that this was what they were thinking in their hearts."

Jesus said to them,

"Why are you thinking these things? Which is easier: to say to the paralytic, 'Your sins are forgiven,' or to say, 'Get up, take your mat and walk'? But that you may know that The Son of Man has authority on earth to forgive sins ..." He says to the man "...get up, take your mat and go home."

Mark's Gospel states that this event took place in Capernaum. In Matthew, it took place in "his own town" while Luke does not specify where the miracle occurred. (See Matthew 9:1-8; Mark 2:1-12; and Luke 5: 17-28).

Apostle Paul in Acts 16 commanded the spirit of divination out of the slave girl, and she was instantly delivered. He didn't negotiate or beg the foul spirit.

"One day as we were going down to the place of prayer, we met a slave girl who had a spirit that enabled her to tell the future. She earned a lot of money for her masters by telling fortunes. She followed Paul and the rest of us, shouting, "These men are servants of the Most High God, and they have come to tell you how to be saved."

This went on day after day until Paul got so exasperated and he turned and said to the demon within her, *"I command you in the name of Jesus Christ to come out of her." And instantly it left her."* (vss 16-18) NLT

The lame man sitting at the Beautiful Gate of the temple in Acts of the Apostles chapter 3 wouldn't have received his powerful miracle of healing if Peter hadn't gathered the courage to command his healing. Again, please notice that Peter and John did not set up a committee to deliberate if it was the will of God for the man, neither did they stop for a second to beg the sickness to leave him. What did they do? They 'said' to him, "we don't have any money on us, but hang on a minute, we will give you what we have." The word was spoken and then Peter helped him up by taking his right hand, and that was it!

Peter and John went to the Temple one afternoon to take part in the three o'clock prayer service. As they approached the Temple, a man lame from birth was being carried in. Each day he was put beside the Temple gate, the one called the Beautiful Gate, so he could beg from the people going into the Temple. When he saw Peter and John about to enter, he asked them for some money.

Peter and John looked at him intently, and Peter said, "Look at us!" The lame man looked at them eagerly, expecting some money. But Peter said, "I don't have any silver or gold for you. But I'll give you what I have. In the name of Jesus Christ, the Nazarene, get up and walk!"

Then Peter took the lame man by the right hand and helped him up. And as he did, the man's feet and ankles were instantly healed and strengthened. He jumped up, stood on his feet, and began to walk! Then, walking, leaping, and praising God, he went into the Temple with them.

All the people saw him walking and heard him praising God. When they realized he was the lame beggar they had seen so often at the Beautiful Gate, they were absolutely astounded! They all rushed out in amazement to Solomon's Colonnade, where the man was holding tightly to Peter and John.

What you say determines your future

Can I make it very clear; what we say will determine our destiny. It is as simple as that. Solomon said:

"A man will be satisfied with good by the fruit of his mouth,
And the recompense of a man's hands will be rendered to him."
(Proverbs 12:14)

When you work, you receive wages, that's part of the results of your labours. Work will determine your future. If you don't work, then you will have a bad future. It's just that simple. Yet God said that your tongue can produce the same kind of result as the work of your hands. Solomon is saying that a man is filled with good things by the fruit of his lips. If you had a choice between having good things or bad things, wouldn't you choose the good things? Of course, you would. Well, how do you get the good things? By the fruit of your lips. Let's look at another scripture which echoes this truth:

"A man shall eat well by the fruit of his mouth, But the soul of the unfaithful feeds on violence." Proverbs 13:2

How does a person enjoy good things and eat well? By the fruit of their lips.

Proverb 18:20-21 also says,

"A man's stomach shall be satisfied from the fruit of his mouth;
From the produce of his lips, he shall be filled. Death and
life are in the power of the tongue, and those who love it will eat
its fruit."

What you say out of your mouth, especially during trying times is going to determine whether you have life or death. Your words determine whether you are going to have blessings or curses. When the Bible speaks of the tongue, it is not referring to the pink, wet, slimy muscle in your mouth. It is referring to the words that the tongue speaks. The tongue is a muscle of speech. It is speech that is powerful, not the muscle itself.

This scripture says that the tongue produces fruit. Let me say it this way: your words produce fruit, and fruit is the end result of seeds. If you hold in your hand an apple, then you hold the result of a seed. So, fruit is the end result of a seed. This means that your words are initially seeds. What you plant now, you will get later. So, what you say now, you will get later. You better watch what you say, because if it is bad, you will reap it. This is one of the most powerful truths that you can learn when it comes to successful living. Every seed holds the promise of tomorrow and tomorrow is the future. So, every seed holds the promise of the future. The life you are living now is the result of the words you spoke in the past. Believe me when I say it.

I've heard parents say, "We don't understand why our kids didn't turn out right. We did everything we could. We even warned them. We told them that they were never going to amount to anything. We told them that they were going to be failures…and they were."
Do you see what these parents did? They constantly spoke negative things to their children. They predicted the future of their children by their words.
You are supposed to warn your children when they do wrong, but you are not supposed to predict that they are going to have a bad future in doing so.

My mother, before she got saved, and a little after, was in the habit of doing this. I warned her one day, "Don't rain curses on your children in the name of correcting them. You can correct them without doing this. Bless, don't curse." She caught my view. After your child has done something wrong, you can correct them and then say, "Honey, what you did was wrong. Jesus lives in you, so you can do better next time, let the Lord live through you. I forgive you." That's better than saying in anger and fear, "you're never going to amount to anything! Are you very sure that I am your parent? I won't be any bit surprised to find you in prison somebody!"

If you've had an upbringing filled with such declarations, I want you to hear this, you can overcome the negative curses by the power of the Lord! What do you do then? Don't believe them. Believe God's report instead. Please read these passages now: 1 John 5:5, Matt 19:26, 1John 4:4, Proverbs 24:16, and Romans 8:28.

Start speaking God's word, and don't repeat the negative words of others, even if those were your parents. Love your parents, respect them, and be kind to them, but don't believe their negative reports about you.

We learn a lesson from the book of Numbers 14. The Israelites grumbled against Moses and Aaron and prophesied doom and gloom on themselves and their children, declaring that they and their children would die in the desert and not enter the Promised Land then God spoke to Moses and told him to give them this message:

"As surely as I live, declares the Lord, I will do to you the very things I heard you say" Numbers 14:28

The Lord told them that they will get what they said about themselves. God did however, exempt the children:

"As for your children that you said will be taken as plunder, I will bring them in to enjoy the land you have rejected" Numbers 14:31

So, you see that your parents' words do not have to determine your destiny, except if YOU let them.

Proverbs 18:21 says that the tongue can produce both life and death. It can be an instrument of good and of bad. The tongue is neutral. It's neither good nor bad; it's only an instrument. The same thing I always say about money and wealth. Money isn't evil, you see. It only becomes bad in the hands of a bad person.

You can use the tongue, your words, to produce good things or you can use it to produce bad. The choice is yours. Your tongue even has the power of health.

"The tongue that brings healing is a tree of life" Prov.15:4
"Reckless words pierce like a sword, but the tongue of the wise brings healing" (Prov. 12:18)
Your tongue can make you well.

God says to decide and decree a thing, and you'll get it. We must do more than "decide" we must "decree."
"You will also declare a thing, and it will be established for you; So, light will shine on your ways." Job 22:28

A decree is a proclamation made by someone with authority. A decree is always made by Kings. A king makes a decree by declaring what is legal and what is illegal, and everyone must obey it, his words are law. His words determine the future of his domain.

Jesus said,

"I tell you the truth, whatever you bind on earth will be bound in heaven, and whatever you lose on earth will be loosed in heaven"
(Matt. 18:18)

The word 'bind' means to declare unlawful. The word 'loose' means to declare lawful. How do we bind and loose? Through our declarations! We declare with our mouths.

Que sera, sera
When I was just a little girl
I asked my mother, "What will I be?
Will I be pretty, will I be rich?"
Here's what she said to me

"Que Sera, Sera
Whatever will be, will be
The future's not ours to see
Que Sera, Sera
What will be, will be"

When I grew up, I fell in love
I asked my sweetheart, "What lies ahead?
Will we have rainbows, day after day?"
Here's what my sweetheart said

"Que Sera, Sera
Whatever will be, will be
The future's not ours, to see
Que Sera, Sera
What will be, will be"

Now I have children of my own
They ask their mother, "What will I be
Will I be handsome, will I be rich?"
I tell them tenderly

"Que Sera, Sera
Whatever will be, will be
The future's not ours, to see
Que Sera, Sera
What will be, will be
Que Sera, Sera."

Songwriters: EVANS RAYMOND B / LIVINGSTON JAY
Que Sera Sera lyrics © Jay Livingston Music, St. Angelo Music, JAY LIVINGSTON
MUSIC INC, ST ANGELO MUSIC

Do you remember this song by the legendary Doris Day? She was no doubt fabulous and one of the greatest stars of her time, we will truly miss her. *"Que Sera, Sera, whatever will be will be"*.

The song became very popular so much so that we forgot to pay attention to the lyrics. I don't argue about the song, but I would like to talk about the real meaning and implication of the main line, at least what we have come to make of it. I have quite a different view about the ideology.

I have chosen to talk about it to drive home a point. The confessions we make, especially when things don't go right with us and what we say about ourselves and about our future affect our life and indeed the direction of our life going forward. Believe it or not, if you leave your life to fate, you won't do anything to speak to your future. If you just resign to the fact that whatever will be, will be, then you can't speak up powerfully against dark and ugly situations brought on by the enemy.

Remember the experience of the prophet Ezekiel? it was as if the conversation went this way *"Ezekiel, it's not up to Me, it's up to you to do something about these bones and see to it that they live"*. I believe Ezekiel was being told by God how to do powerful confessions when in need of a breakthrough.

Your talk is your future. In fact, the life you are living today is the exact picture you painted with your words yesterday. Your tongue is the director of your life. Where your tongue goes, you go. If your tongue is confused, your life will be confused.

I believe that your future is not just in your hands but in your mouth, and it's up to you to speak it into existence.

The story of the cursing of the fig tree lends a pattern to us. In the gospel of Mark, chapter eleven Jesus spoke aloud to the fig tree which was an acted-out parable related to the clearing of the temple. The tree showed promise of fruit, but it produced none. Jesus was showing His anger at religious life without substance. If you claim to have faith without putting it to work in your life, you are like the barren fig tree.

Fig trees, a popular source of inexpensive food in Israel, require three years from the time they are planted until they can bear fruit. Each tree yields a great amount of fruit twice a year, in late spring and in early autumn. This incident occurred early in the spring when the leaves were beginning to bud. The figs normally grow as the leaves fill out, but this tree, though full of leaves, had no figs. The tree looked promising but offered no fruit. The Lord expected to get some fruits from the tree but was disappointed. He had seen the tree from a distance and then drew closer. That meant he was far from His disciples.

Sometimes we don't confess God's word because we want to make sure no one really knows what they believe. If you are going to see the obstacle removed, you must be ready to confess powerfully with God's word in prayer. If you make any provision for failure, then the answer is not guaranteed.

Most people believe that God will heal them. After all, I have rebuked the devil, so I know I'm going to be healed, they say. But I also believe that if I die, I'm going to be with the Lord, they conclude. This sounds good, but these people are making provision for failure. Jesus did not make room for failure; He was always serious with spiritual issues. For me, there are times to get aggressive in the spirit and speak against the wiles of the devil.

Many years ago, during the days of the Methodist charismatic/evangelical uprising in Nigeria, I was at the forefront as a young man leading revivals and renewal services and the Lord moved mightily in salvation, healing, signs, and wonders. There were quite sometimes when it went really wild that you could call it 'spiritual chaos', it was just like scenes from the Acts of the Apostles. One day, after one of these services, I was confronted by a church elder. He said to me, 'why do you encourage people to shout and make noise, Jesus said to go to your inner room and quietly pray to your heavenly father who sees in secret,' and I remember saying to him, 'sir, Jesus also shouted when the situation called for it, so I endorse the shouts and claps during prayer and worship.' He went away bowing his face and accusing me of bringing in 'foreign' teachings to our 'orderly' church.

Chapter Four
Overcoming Fear and Anxiety Through Prayer

"Are not five sparrows sold for two copper coins? And not one of them is forgotten before God. ⁷ But the very hairs of your head are all numbered. Do not fear; therefore, you are of more value than many sparrows." Luke 12:6,7

Fear is defined as *'an unpleasant emotion caused by the threat of danger, pain or harm.'* When I was in the University, a friend of mine defined fear with the acronym F.E.A.R.- *False Evidence Appearing Real* or *False Experiences Appearing Real.* In the real sense, there are many things which we are afraid of, but they are mere false experiences.

Fear and anxiety can cause many problems for a believer. They will clutter your spirit and can kill your dreams, thus derailing your destiny. The decision not to fear is up to you. Fear is negative, and may come with anxiety, depression, and many other dark elements. Fear is the key that opens the door to other spirits that cause the destructions and disasters that people will experience.

We can identify two strands of fear in the Bible. 'The fear of the Lord' and 'the spirit of fear.' I can say that 'the fear of the Lord' is a reverential awe of God, respect for His power and glory.

"The fear of the Lord is the beginning of wisdom; A good understanding have all those who do His commandments. His praise endures forever." Psalm 111:10

The spirit of fear is harmful because it can become a stronghold. These can be fearful thoughts, fear of the unknown or anxiety. Uncertainty and anxiety about yourself and your identity, a feeling of insecurity, maybe in your relationship. Some people even refuse to go to bed at night just because of fear! We may indeed worry about things that haven't happened which may never happen, things like sickness, accident, stillbirth, even death. Fear could also impact on our physical health. It is a worry and something of concern when you are continuously apprehensive, and always expecting something bad to happen, for you it is not if, but when. As you do this, you are gripped by a feeling of self-doubt and a lack of confidence. Fear is a bondage and is filled with torment.

What are the things that can trigger fear in the life of a believer? A past ugly experience could be a trigger for fear. We could also become fearful because of past negative words spoken over us, especially by authority figures in our lives. A lack of faith in the word of God could also cause fear. Whenever fear comes in, remember that God will stay with you through difficult times and that He has promised you great blessings in His word as His beloved. God's blessings are beyond our imaginations. It was Abram's belief in the Lord, not his actions that made him right with God (Genesis 15:5).

Can fear be useful?

I believe that fear could be useful. How do you mean, you may ask? When you are afraid or simply apprehensive, this could help you avoid a repeat of past mistakes by making you cautious. Fear could be a motivation for better performance, it can help you escape danger of being cheated or bullied. It could help you prepare for an oncoming challenge. Fear could be healthy sometimes, have ever wondered why we keep our houses locked and windows closed at night while we sleep? Before we cross the road, we look left and right and when we buy groceries, we make sure to read through the stickers and labels before consuming them.

As believers, there are many things that can tempt us into fear. You must understand that fear is a state, not an impulse. For example, when you see a snake, you may get shocked at the sudden sight of the snake. Now it remains for you to either snap out of that unconscious phase that is supposed to pass or remain in it and build a mindset that makes the snake more powerful than yourself; it is totally up to you.

When a believer is faced with diverse conditions and situations, he is excused to panic at first, because honestly, we are still human. However, it begins to become a matter of concern if this believer builds a camp around that state and makes fear a tenant.

If a believer becomes this person that is subject to the fear that may arise from any condition at all, then we begin to question what they have known and what they believe in.

The Bible teaches us that we have the ability to overcome anything and everything that can cause us to remain in a state of fear. The real deal is how we react to fear. Let us learn to understand our fears, this will teach us to control or use our fears.

There is nothing that the power of God cannot overcome in and through us.

We know that there are many things in our world today that can cause fear and anxiety. For example, the global pandemic that struck our world and indeed changed everything we have known which, I'm sure you will believe me, has really put an end the word, as we knew. It was scary at first and rightly so but should not be so forever. As believers, we should know that God is our Father, and we have His protection. God is able to heal our diseases by the stripes of Jesus no matter where these diseases have originated from:

"Who Himself bore our sins in His body on the tree, that we, having died to sins, might live for righteousness - by whose stripes you were healed." 1 Peter 2:24

God is also able to in fact protect us from the disease before we get sick. (Psalms 91).

One thing you need to do is to feed your mind with the scriptures instead of bad reports, news, and gossips. Have a disciplined mind. We might not avoid thoughts, but we certainly can control them by a disciplined mind. So, learn to discipline your mind to think faith instead of fear.

Praying fear away

It is extremely important for a believer to know these things and begin to proclaim and enforce them through the ministry of prayer.

Your prayer points do not just come out of nowhere or out of your will, but in fact, they are an expression of the will of God through His word.

What do we mean by faith? Some people get confused on the whole idea and function of faith. Faith is useless without the will of God. No matter how much faith anyone may claim to possess, if what they pray for or declare cannot be found in the eternal written word of God and proven to be consistent with God's character, then God is not obliged to answer that prayer.

This is why we are able to confidently pray for things like salvation, healing, boldness, prosperity, and the things that we have found to be the will of God, because that is our "faith" – that He will hear and answer.

This is the same with the issue of fear, we know that it is God's will for the people who are called by His name not to be slaves to fear. So, we have the boldness to pray against every spirit of fear, because it is contrary to the will of God.

The word of God tells us of how much God desires to save men from the bondage of fear, and this took Him to the extent of putting Himself in man as the only and ultimate way to make this possible. The Bible says in Romans 8:15:

"For you did not receive the spirit of bondage again to fear, but you received the Spirit of adoption by which we cry out, "Abba, Father.""

Formerly, we were subject to fear when we were not partakers of the divine nature. The natural man is always afraid of everything - fear of death, of sicknesses and diseases, fear of lack. Oh, what a life of depressing thought – they fear all manner of things that the devil inflicts on them. This is why as children of God, we cannot fear these things again, because of the presence of God's Spirit in us.

You have God living in you, what else can defeat you? Fear is one of the biggest enemies that God put under the feet of Jesus, so we have victory over it.

Again, the scripture says:

"For God has not given us a spirit of fear, but of power and of love and of a sound mind." 2 Timothy 1:7

There it is again, "The spirit of power, and of love, and of a sound mind." We are really blessed by the grace of God!

Fear and anxiety are far below what Christ died to give us. We have a duty as believers to enforce that victory of Christ through the legal system of prayer. God is aware that even the most Spirit-filled believer can be tempted into seasons of fear and anxiety, so Paul encourages the church saying:

"Be not anxious for nothing, but in everything by prayer and supplication, with thanksgiving, let your requests be made known to God." Philippians 4:6

That's it! Paul encourages the church to be confident in the provision and salvation of their God, engaging His power in prayer. He says, *"Do not be anxious…"*, which means that we can be anxious if we choose to let fear have its way. But we must continually bring all our supplications and prayers to God, with the heart of thanksgiving; knowing that God is able to and is going to do it.

We must trust in the power of God first. That is the faith that God wants; that we know what He can do, and then believe and wait for Him to do it. The book of Hebrews says:

"But without faith it is impossible to please Him, for he who comes to God must believe that He is, and that He is a rewarder of those who diligently seek Him." Hebrews 11:6

Praying without ceasing is the duty of a believer that wants to overcome any kind of fear. (1 Thessalonians 5:17).

Let us continue to pray even if it seems like things are not changing. The character of faith is not praying once and receiving the answers immediately, but that even when the clouds are not forming, we continue to be on our knees and wait for it to come as Elijah did. The Bible says about the power of fervency in prayer:

"... The effective, fervent prayer of a righteous man avails much. Elijah was a man with a nature like ours, and he prayed earnestly that it would not rain; and it did not rain on the land for three years and six months." James 5:16-17

If you have been praying, and it seems like fear and anxiety lingers, this is not the time to get distracted. Continue to pray until you find peace. The Bible is full of people who continued to pray until they broke-through. That is the character of faith! Have you heard about P.U.S.H? -Pray Until Something Happens. That is how our attitude to prayer ought to be. Persistence works, it worked for the woman with the issue of blood in Matthew 5, it worked for the lepers 2 Kings 7, and it sure will work for you.

You can only find peace from God through the instrument of prayer. That is why we find the apostles continually praying for the church in their letters, speaking of peace always as a prayer over them.

Whatever you are having concerns over, no matter how big and impossible they seem, God is able to calm every storm and deliver you. You just have to be confident and keep praying in faith, because God is faithful and will always come through for His beloved.

Jesus said to cast all your burdens on Him, and the way to do that is surrendering to Him in the place of prayer. (Matthew 11:28; 1 Peter 5:7)

Chapter Five
Knocked Down but Not Defeated

"We are hard-pressed on every side, yet not crushed; we are perplexed, but not in despair; persecuted, but not forsaken; struck down, but not destroyed always carrying about in the body the dying of the Lord Jesus, that the life of Jesus also may be manifested in our body." 2 Corinthians 4:8-10

Boxing is a very interesting competition. It is usually a long title fight made up of what is called the championship distance, divided into (usually 15) rounds and what interests me is the fact that knocking someone down in the first round or any round at all does not necessarily mean that they have been defeated. No fighter is declared a winner or loser until the fight is over. The one who wins a round is not necessarily the one who wins the fight. Even a very powerful fighter may be knocked down in a round but what makes them a great fighter is their ability to rise back on their feet to continue the fight.

Incidentally I have watched with pity when some of the fighters when knocked down in the middle of the fight falls woefully as if they have already lost the contest. They manage to get up on their feet and staggers to their post where the coach and the medical team pours water on their head, cheering them up and encouraging them to go for a win. Surprisingly the same man who had been knocked down is back on his feet for another round of the fight as if nothing happened before.

The Christian experience and indeed life generally is often likened to a boxing contest. I believe that what happens to me is not really a big deal but what I do with what happens to me. It was Plato who said, 'be kind, for everyone you meet is fighting a hard battle.' Life could bring anything our way as long as we live on planet earth, but what do you make out of it? In 1 Timothy 6:12 the Christian is admonished to fight the good fight of faith to obtain eternal life which is the ultimate goal of every Christian. The apostle Paul, when he had the premonition that he had completed his lifespan and was soon to die wrote

"the time has come for my departure, I have fought the good fight, I have finished my race. I have kept the faith" 2 Timothy 2:6-7

Again, in 1st Corinthians chapter 9, verses 25 and 26 the Bible says

"...I do not fight like a man beating the air; so that after I have preached the gospel to others I will not be disqualified."

The fight we are talking about is not the physical exchange of blows.

"For we wrestle not against flesh and blood but against principalities and powers of darkness, against spiritual forces of evil" Eph.6:12

This fight, which is against Satan and his strategies presents itself in form of trials of our faith. In the form of temptations, discouraging situations, spiritual manipulations and circumstances that challenge our faith. Satan usually intends to use the fight to deceive, dissuade, and distract the Christian from the faith. But God's reason for allowing the fight is to boost our faith, to make us stronger and resilient. Any Christian who either does not encounter challenges of life or who gives up the faith in the face of challenges will not experience desirable growth and maturity in his or her faith. Just as a student is promoted after passing the prescribed examinations, so also a Christian grows from strength to strength in their faith by overcoming challenges of life. Each challenge you overcome leads to the advancement of your faith and at the same time becomes a reference point to overcoming another challenge.

One of the strategies to being victorious in this fight is to never give up. The slogan for those who must win is "keep fighting". Any time you are knocked down you must determine to get up and keep fighting. Probably, issues of life have dealt a heavy blow on you. Perhaps you have been knocked down and there is no hope in sight, I urge you to arise and keep fighting. You cannot afford to give up now.

> *"These things I have spoken to you, that in Me you may have peace. In the world you will have tribulation; but be of good cheer, I have overcome the world."* John. 16:33

One passage of scripture that the Holy Spirit gave me during this period is Psalm 34:19,

> *"Many are the afflictions of the righteous, But the Lord delivers him out of them all."*

Are you knocked down by one health challenge or the other? Have you lost your job during the pandemic? Did you lose a piece of property? Did you lose a loved one?

Loss of a loved one is not very easy to bear, especially if the person was really dear to your heart. It could seem like the whole world has turned upside-down. This is a heavy blow that can knock somebody down. However, you are expected to wipe your tears, pick up what is remaining of your life and move on. If there is a situation that has made you to ask, "God why me?" then sure you have been knocked down. Do you feel rejected, forgotten, trampled upon, abused, disgraced, or even betrayed? It means you have received a heavy punch.

When you feel lonely, rejected, and forsaken, Jesus understands your condition. In fact, He is right there quietly with you. He feels what you feel.

Hebrews 4:15; *"for we do not have a high priest who is unable to Sympathize with our weaknesses, but we have one who has been tempted in every way, just as we are – yet without sin."* (NIV)

"for we have not an high priest which cannot be touched with the feeling of our infirmities" (KJV)

Hence Jesus is able to sympathize with us because He is touched with the feeling of our pain. The shortest verse in the Bible says that when Jesus came to the tomb where His friend Lazarus was buried

"Jesus wept" John 11:35

For Jesus to weep, the loss must have been a very painful one. So, if you are knocked down by the demise of a loved one, Jesus understands what it means because He has been there. When I lost my dad, it was like the whole world crashing down on me, he was so dear to us, and we wanted him to live longer to reap the fruits of his labours. The good thing is that he did reap some of it and that he was blood-washed and saved by grace, hallelujah! I remember hearing from folk who came on condolence visit, and they said things like, 'we understand how you feel,' and I said to my mind, 'no you don't!' Some of them even told me that I didn't need their consolation because I was already a Christian leader who should console others, how insensitive!

Probably the people you showed love later turned around with evil machinations, probably the people you trusted so much have turned around to betray you or may be those you expected to help you have deserted and turned their back on you or loved ones deserted you. Jesus understands that too.

In Matthew 26:47 – 49, it was Judas, one of the disciples, in fact the one He trusted so much as to make him the treasurer, a very close confidant who turned around and betrayed Jesus with a kiss.

We could be knocked down by hunger and lack of necessities of life. May be for one reason or the other your daily bread is no longer guaranteed. I assure you Jesus understands you because He has been there. In Matthew 17:24-27, when tax collectors wanted to embarrass him because of payment of taxes, there was no money to settle the arrogant tax collectors. You can imagine what the scenario would look like. But thank God that miraculously some coins were provided to save the situation. So, Jesus understands how it feels.

"When they had come to Capernaum, those who received the temple tax came to Peter and said, "Does your Teacher not pay the temple tax?" He said, "Yes." And when he had come into the house, Jesus anticipated him, saying, "What do you think, Simon? From whom do the kings of the earth take customs or taxes, from their sons or from strangers?" Peter said to Him, "From strangers." Jesus said to him, "Then the sons are free. Nevertheless, lest we offend them, go to the sea, cast in a hook,

and take the fish that comes up first. And when you have opened its mouth, you will find a piece of money; take that and give it to them for Me and you."

Are you suffering with any disease, ailment, infirmity, or anything that cause pain in the body, Jesus has been there too? He received 39 excruciating strokes of the whip. His hands and feet were hammered to the cross, with a crown made of thorns upon His head. The side of His belly was pierced with a spear and water and blood gushed out. He was suspended on the cross until His breath ebbed away. So, He understands what it looks like to have pain in the body.

Did you lose a precious property? Jesus knows the pain of loss. I think if you lost valuables but still have your life, you might still somehow recover and acquire a replacement. I don't think there is any loss greater than the loss of one's life. Jesus sacrificed His life at the age of only 33 years. Although we know that He voluntarily gave His life, but it was not a palatable experience for him. At a time, He had to plead the Father that the "cup" (referring to the suffering and death) should be taken away from Him. Therefore, He understands the pain of loss.
He has since resurrected and ascended into heaven and is pleading our case in the presence of the father. He is a worthy advocate.
Hebrews 4:15 describes Him as the High Priest who can sympathize with us because He can be touched with the feeling of our infirmities. Listen, Jesus is with you right there, so stop feeling lonely and dejected. He understands when you cry. He feels what you feel. He is willing to help if only you can call on him today, and keep calling until help comes, but I assure you, He will come. *"He heals the broken-hearted and binds up their wounds"* Psalm 147:3

2. Corinthians 4:8, 9,

"We are hard pressed on every side, but not crushed; perplexed but not in despair; persecuted but not abandoned; knocked down but not destroyed."

Beloved, as long as there is breath in your nostrils, there is hope. Job 14: 7-9, *"But there is hope for a tree if it is cut down, it will sprout again, and its shoots will not fail. Although its roots may grow old in the ground and its stump begins to die in the soil, at the scent of water it will flourish and put forth shoots like a new plant."*

Are you still alive? Then you must have to bounce back on your feet and fight back. Keep fighting till you win. Giving up will be a very costly mistake. Yes, you may have been knocked down, but you are not destroyed. The prize fighter's bell hasn't gone yet, hence it is not yet over. It is not over until it is over!

One of my favourite scriptures is,

"For the lovers of God may suffer adversity and stumble seven times, but they will continue to rise over and over again. But the unrighteous are brought down by just one calamity and will never be able to rise again." Proverbs 24:16 (TPT)

Chapter Six
Knowing Who You Are in Christ

"Therefore, if anyone is in Christ, he is a new creation; old things have passed away; behold, all things have become new" 2 Corinthians 5:17

When you accepted Jesus Christ as your Saviour, all your sins were forgiven. Every sin you had committed was redeemed by the death of Jesus Christ on the cross,
"I write to you, little children, because your sins are forgiven you for His name's sake" 1 John 2:12

The choice of following Jesus made the devil furious, which means you left him to join the individuals who have a place with the Lord Jesus. Also, any individual who attempts to live for Jesus Christ will rapidly be assaulted and enticed by Satan. Satan cannot take you from the family of God, yet he will do everything he can to discourage you. He will attempt to make you question your salvation. He will try to convince you to believe that you won't ever have the power to resist temptations. He will attempt to make you question God's love for you. But God has started a good work in you, and you can be sure that He will continue to do it.

"being confident of this very thing, that He who has begun a good work in you will complete it until the day of Jesus Christ;" Philippians 1:6

When you become a Christian, you are actually born of the water and the Spirit. A man called Nicodemus was already a prominent religious leader among the Jews and was part of the sect called the Pharisees, yet he was unsaved, when he met Jesus, He told him,

"Jesus answered, "Most assuredly, I say to you, unless one is born of water and the Spirit, he cannot enter the kingdom of God." John 3:5

Water, for some people represents the Word of God, it is through our encounter with the revealed Word that we are made aware of our need for salvation.

"that He might sanctify and cleanse her with the washing of water by the word," Ephesians 5:26

God's word is still very relevant and powerful today, I believe it is inerrant. The Word sanctifies, the Word cleanses. To some others, water represents baptism, through which we are welcomed into the body of Christ. And the Spirit? It is not our intelligence that converts a soul, no matter how powerful and eloquent you think you are, salvation is the work of the Holy Spirit of God, but we have to do our part,

"How then shall they call on Him in whom they have not believed? And how shall they believe in Him of whom they have not heard? And how shall they hear without a preacher? And how shall they preach unless they are sent? As it is written: "How beautiful are the feet of those who preach the gospel of peace, who bring glad tidings of good things!" Romans 10:14,15

It is wickedness to refuse to share the good news when you have received it yourself. Sharing the gospel has been described as the thing that happens when a beggar tells another beggar where to find food. There are so many people around us hungry, starving and dying, for the food of life, we don't need to travel far away into Africa to become some sort of missionaries today, the world is now at our doorsteps! And in fact, I can boldly say that Africa and The Global South are now the major sending nations. Europe and indeed the West have now become a missionary ground. We are a post-Christian secularized society. Secularism and post-modern thought are the order of the day. We are so rapidly turning our backs to the faith of our fathers so much so that many people whose parents were very active Christians are today promoting irreligion, including humanism and atheism.

The number of people in Britain who say they have no religion has increased by a staggering percentage over the past few years, making non-religious people the fastest growing group in the country, according to the Office of National Statistics (ONS). The data from the ONS, taken from the Annual Population Survey, show the number of non-religious people has increased by nearly a half since the last Census with more than 8 million more people now saying they have no religion. The results also showed a steady decline in the number of people who say they are Christians and a steady growth in other groups like Muslim, Jewish and Hindu. Humanists UK, the national charity working on behalf of non-religious people, raised concerns about the leading question used in the survey which asked, 'What is your religion?' It has been advocating for the Census question and other survey questions on religion and belief to change to 'What is your religion, if any? They are now seriously calling on the Government to take heed of the latest figures by better representing non-religious people in government policies. Nevertheless, I believe that revival is coming, and we are surely part of it, amen!

We must remember that as Christians, we worship the God who is Spirit.

"God is Spirit, and those who worship Him must worship in spirit and truth." John 4:24

How we worship is more important to Him than *where* we worship. Because He is Spirit, we can in essence worship Him from anywhere, but it has to be 'in spirit and truth'. In spirit, that is to say it has to be according to His own nature, and in the truth of the everlasting Word. I am not saying any other thing other than that denominations and church groups are not anything He worries about but sincere worship. What is His nature, you may like to ask? He has made us in His nature.

Before we arrived here on earth, God had prepared everything and created everything so we could be comfortable and have dominion. God's nature is that of dominion and authority, so that is what we share in. And again, don't get me wrong when I say dominion, because I don't believe that God told us to lord it over His creation, but to cultivate and look after it. We must be accountable because we are co-creators with Him. I am very passionate about the theme of eco-justice and care for the earth!

"The Lord God took the man and put him in the Garden of Eden to work it and take care of it." Genesis 2:15 (NIV)

When God finished all creation, He saw that they were all good, then God said, 'let us' make man in our own image. This may be referring to the Trinity because 'us' in Genesis chapter One means 'ELOHIM' in the Hebrew language which means 'one true God.' Another view about this is that the plural wording is used to denote majesty. Kings traditionally use the plural form in speaking of themselves. Yet another school of thought believe that God was referring to the heavenly beings, but I strongly think that the passage talks of the Trinity.

"Then God said, "Let us make mankind in our image, in our likeness, so that they may rule over the fish in the sea and the birds in the sky, over the livestock and all the wild animals, and over all the creatures that move along the ground." Genesis 1:26

It was only while creating humans that ELOHIM overall were involved and they 'came down'. God did not just speak a word as He had done in when He was creating the heavens and the earth and everything that is in it. That means we are not just ordinary users, but joint heirs with Christ.
The believer is royalty. We are 'gods' as the psalmist says.

"I said, "You are gods, and all of you are children of the Most High." Psalm 82:6. Our saviour Jesus Christ referred to this verse, "Jesus answered them, "Is it not written in your law, 'I said, "You are gods" '? If He called them gods, to whom the word of God came (and the Scripture cannot be broken), do you say of Him whom the Father sanctified and sent into the world, 'You are blaspheming,' because I said, 'I am the Son of God'?" John 10:34-36

When God finished all creation, He saw that they were all good, then God said, 'let us make man in our own image'. Being created in the image of God doesn't mean we look like God in the physical sense, we are the image of God in character, control, power and dominion.

"Behold, I give you the authority to trample on serpents and scorpions, and over all the power of the enemy, and nothing shall by any means hurt you. Nevertheless, do not rejoice in this, that the spirits are subject to you, but rather rejoice because your names are written in heaven." Luke 10:19,20

We are 'judges'

The Hebrew word ELOHIM is translated as 'a judge' sometimes in the Bible. Both in Psalm 82:6 and in John 10:34, it could be translated as 'judges', 'mighty ones', 'a ruler' or 'gods.' They all are used for people who hold positions of authority and rule. It is also translated as judge in Exodus 21:6; 22:8, 9, 28.

You have the seed of God

We are created with the seed of God in us. Remember that the Bible says that Jesus is the second Adam, it was through Adam that man lost his dominion and authority but through our new birth through Jesus Christ authority and dominion are restored. Believers have the seed of God, the very life of God called 'Zoe.'

"Whoever has been born of God does not sin, for His seed remains in him; and he cannot sin, because he has been born of God." 1 John 3:9. The real meaning of this sentence 'does not sin' actually means 'does not make a practice of sin.' Look at the Amplified version, *"No one who is born of God [deliberately, knowingly, and habitually] practices sin, because God's seed [His principle of life, the essence of His righteous character] remains [permanently] in him [who is born again—who is reborn from above spiritually transformed, renewed, and set apart for His purpose]; and he [who is born again] cannot habitually [live a life characterized by] sin, because he is born of God and longs to please Him."*

You are eternal

When God breathe His spirit in us after creation, that means we are now eternal. If you know this, it will inform the way you live on earth. When we die, we just transition from here into eternity, we don't cease to exist. It should be very concerning to you to prepare yourself for where you will spend eternity. Heaven is real and hell fire is also real, the choice is yours and you must make that choice now. When you are born again, your body and your mind remain the same, but your spirit is recreated. Even though the initial peace and joy of salvation affect your way of thinking, basically, your mind is still in the same condition. It is obvious that all your old thoughts didn't pass away, because you still remember the same things you did before you were saved. If you were tall, with big head before you repented, you still are. My point is, the new birth is a spiritual experience which changes the human spirit from being dead and separated from God to a live spirit who fellowships with God, it happens in an instant, but the salvation of your mind and soul is a progressive story and requires a conscious effort on your side. You cannot improve the salvation of your spirit, you can't add to it, you can't make it better, except to receive it. Salvation is a gift; it is not of works. But you still have a soul and live in a body, these are not saved.

The Bible says in 2 Corinthians 5:17 *"Therefore, if anyone is in Christ, he is a new creation; old things have passed away; behold, all things have become new."*

You may not fully realize this, but you are a spirit because the real you in not your body. The key to a successful Christian life is to get your mind to line up with the Holy Spirit and obey what your spirit man says.

"For to be carnally minded is death, but to be spiritually minded is life and peace. Because the carnal mind is enmity against God; for it is not subject to the law of God, nor indeed can be." Romans 8: 6,7

Sometimes our thinking and reasoning can reject the information given by our spirit and we continue to do our own thing. It is possible to be saved and still be conformed to the patterns of the world, when this happens, the individual will not enjoy the Christian life. When the Apostle said to renew our mind, he was not writing to sinners but the church in Rome.

"And do not be conformed to this world, but be transformed by the renewing of your mind, that you may prove what is that good and acceptable and perfect will of God." Romans 12:2

They were men and women who knew the Lord Jesus as Saviour and were operating in the gifts of the Spirit, yet Paul warned them not to be conformed to this world.

The mind is part of your soul, it must be transformed. It must be renewed. It must be changed. This is not done by learning, but by changing. You must commit to constant study, discipline, confession, conversation; your thinking must be constantly renewed. It takes change to grow in the spirit and it takes growth to walk with God. To 'renew' our mind is from Greek word *Anakainoo* which means to make new or to change your thinking to God's thought. It is a never-ending process. Like Gaius, you must work every day and every hour to renew your mind. You must be in a constant process of changing your way of thinking to be able to do God's will.

"Beloved, I pray that you may prosper in all things and be in health, just as your soul prospers. For I rejoiced greatly when

brethren came and testified of the truth that is in you, just as you walk in the truth. I have no greater joy than to hear that my children walk in truth." 3 John 2-4

You have unlimited treasure in you

If you have got the *zoe* life in you, that simply means you have a hidden treasure of possibilities residing inside of you. *"For it is the God who commanded light to shine out of darkness, who has shone in our hearts to give the light of the knowledge of the glory of God in the face of Jesus Christ. But we have this treasure in earthen vessels, that the excellence of the power may be of God and not of us."* 2 Corinthians 4:6,7

If it is impossible for God to fail, then you are called to be above and not beneath. When things go wrong, I want you to go back to God and plead for divine intervention, He will come through for you. We serve a God of miracles, a God who is an impossibilities' specialist.

A little lower than ELOHIM

Let us look at this passage again,
"What is man that You are mindful of him,
*And the son of man that You visit him? For You have made him **a***
***little lower than the angels**,*
And You have crowned him with glory and honour. You have made him to have dominion over the works of Your hands; You have put all things under his feet, all sheep and oxen—Even the beasts of the field, the birds of the air, And the fish of the sea That pass through the paths of the seas." Psalm 8:4-8 (emphasis mine)

You are made a little lower than ELOHIM and not the angels. What the King James version missed out is that when you are created with God's image and likeness, you are in fact made a little lower than ELOHIM 'for a time.' Let's read this passage from The Passion Translation,

*"Why would you bother with puny, mortal man or care about human beings? Yet what honour you have given to men, **created only a little lower than Elohim**, crowned with glory and magnificence. You have delegated to them rulership over all you have made, with everything under their authority, placing earth itself under the feet of your image-bearers. All the created order and every living thing of the earth, sky, and sea—the wildest beasts and all that move in the paths of the sea—everything is in submission to Adam's sons."*

The dignity and power that Adam lost through the fall were reclaimed by our Lord Jesus Christ, the second Adam and these became ours through the new covenant, that's why I said we are joint creators with God. We cannot be made lower than the angels because the angels are only servants and ministering spirits sent to serve the re-created man by accompanying and protecting them. (see Hebrews 1:14). And the apostle Paul mentions that we will indeed judge the angels.

"Do you not know that we shall judge angels? How much more, things that pertain to this life?" 1 Corinthians 6:3

God wants you to know that you have been saved

"And this is the testimony: that God has given us eternal life, and this life is in His Son. He who has the Son has life; he who does not have the Son of God does not have life." 1 John 5:11-12

One of the principal things Satan will do after you are saved is to attempt to make you question your salvation. But as a child of God, you should know and have the affirmation that you are saved. By the Word of God, we know that we are saved, not by our feelings. Our feelings change every day, but the Word of God is still the same. God says that if Jesus Christ is your Saviour, you have eternal life. You are saved because God says so in His Word. Nothing can take us from the hands of God. The Lord Jesus saves us, yet He likewise keeps us. He refers to us as His "sheep," and He guarantees that we will never perish (John 10:27-28). The word "perish" means to be lost. Jesus says we won't ever be lost. Jesus discloses to us that we have His abundant life. Nobody can at any point take us from the powerful hands of God (John 10:29). Righteousness is often misunderstood. This is what God has to say about it:

For our sake He made Him to be sin who knew no sin, so that in Him we might become the righteousness of God. (2 Corinthians 5:21)

Dikaiosune

The Greek root of the word translated "righteousness" in this verse also appears in Romans 5:1 with the English translation reading "having been justified." It has come from a Greek root word called *"dikaiosune."*

Therefore, since we have been justified by faith, we have peace with God through our Lord Jesus Christ. Through Him we have also obtained access by faith into this grace in which we stand, and we rejoice in hope of the glory of God. Romans 5:1-2

"Righteousness" refers to our position before God.

Because Jesus lived a perfect life, those who believe in Him are no longer objects of God's wrath but are instead declared right with God because we are clothed in Christ's righteousness as sons and daughters of the living God.

I have a unique way of explaining my point. Let us imagine that a pregnant lady comes to visit you. She knocks on your door wanting to come in to visit you and when you open your door, you say to her, "I know you, so you can come in, but because I don't know the baby, can you leave him outside as you come in, please"? That's insanity, isn't it? The baby in the womb is automatically invited if the mother is invited in. That is righteousness, right standing with God.

Being a daughter or son of God has a multitude of implications that we'll keep on learning our whole lives long. There a one or two pertinent points to always remember:

You have a Father
Romans 8:15 tells us that we have received the Spirit of adoption by whom we cry out, *"Abba, Father."* We are not orphans without the provision and protection of a loving Father.

You are part of a family
In John 1:12 we see that all who receive Jesus Christ are given the right to become children of God. According to Ephesians 2:19 we are members of the household of God. We have brothers and sisters who support us, work alongside us, and encourage us in our faith, as we do the same for them.

You are an heir

The child of a king is an heir to his kingdom, and the Bible informs us that's the case for the daughters and sons of the King of Kings. In Galatians 4:7 we read that if we are sons of God, we are also heirs of God through Christ. This means that we will enjoy the riches of Christ for eternity.

You are a saint

It is sad that our culture has twisted the term saint from its true biblical meaning. We often think of a saint as someone who is perfect, which can make us hesitant to claim that identity for ourselves. Sometimes also we think these are venerated individuals. But I Corinthians 1:2 the Bible reveals that a saint is simply one who is in the process of being made holy because God has set them apart from the world. By His grace, you are a child of God, a saint who has been made righteous in Christ.

Your identity is secured His grace

Ephesians 2:8 tells us plainly that it is by God's grace that we're saved through faith, and not of our own doing. This is because our very best efforts on our very best days amount to filthy rags (Isaiah 64:6). Not only that, but in Jeremiah 17:9, God tells us that our hearts are deceitful above all things, and desperately wicked.

It is plainly impossible to have a healthy identity based on your own merit? God knew that apart from His intervention, we are utterly without hope. It's only because of His grace that we're able to claim our new identity in Christ.

God wants you to understand that you can conquer temptation

"No temptation has overtaken you except such as is common to man; but God is faithful, who will not allow you to be tempted beyond what you are able, but with the temptation will also make the way of escape, that you may be able to bear it" 1 Corinthians 10:13

Here is another way the devil can attack you. He can put various thoughts in your mind that make you feel defeated. Here too, our weapon to defeat satan is the Word of God. Here are things you should know when you are in temptation:

1. Other people are tempted by the same things as you.
2. God always does what He promised, and you can count on the faithfulness of God.
3. God promised that He would not allow you to be tempted beyond what you can bear.
4. God will always prepare a way to escape temptation so that you don't have to sin.

Satan sometimes tries to make us think that we have sinned just because we have been tempted to do terrible things. But temptation in itself is not sin. The only time we sin is when we give in to temptations. Despite being tempted several times, the Lord Jesus never sinned. You will be tempted as long as you live in this world, but with God's support, you will conquer temptation. God will give you the strength to overcome temptation, so that you do not sin (John 16:33).

God wants you to know that He is ready to forgive you whenever you sin

"If we confess our sins, He is faithful and just to forgive us our sins and to cleanse us from all unrighteousness." 1 John 1:9

Indeed, we do not have to sin, and it is correct that we still have a sinful nature, and we often succumb (1 John 1.8). Satan immediately comes to condemn us when we sin. As Christians, we should know that once we feel remorse and confess our sins, the Word of God says that He is faithful and righteous to forgive us. It doesn't matter how many times we succumb; God promises to forgive us if we confess our sins to Him. God does not love our sins, but He loves us. His love for us never changes. God adores all individuals; however, He has an uncommon love for His children. God loves us since we have a place with Jesus Christ. At the point when God looks at us, He sees us "in Christ." God loves us as He cherishes His own Son (John 16.27).

God wants you to know that He hears and answers your prayers

"Until now you have asked nothing in My name. Ask, and you will receive, that your joy may be full." John 16:24

Becoming a Christian does not mean that we will never have problems. Of course, the Bible has already warned us that we would have many issues and troubles in this world. When you have a big problem, Satan tries to discourage you, he tries to make you doubt the love and faithfulness of God. But the Bible says that God is our heavenly Father and that He hears and answers the prayers of His children. God loves us, and He wants us to come to him with our problems (1 Peter 5:7).

When we are in need, we should pray to the Father in the name of Jesus. Jesus taught us that God is truly our Father. We have to come to Him and ask Him what we need (John 16:24). God does not promise to answer our prayers if we have sin in our life that we do not want to give up. But if we do what pleases Him, God will give us what we ask for (1 John 3:22).

Thinking about all the beautiful things Christ has done for you, you should love Christ with all your heart, this is exactly what Christ wants you to do. Jesus loves you, and He wants you to love Him (1 John 4:19). To love Christ is to give Him the first place in your life. One of the things that make us know that we are truly saved is that we have an undying desire to please God. Below are some ways to please God, if at all:

I. When we love Him (Matthew 22:37).
II. When we study His Word and pray to him (John 15.7).
III. When we obey him (1 John 5.3).
IV. When we trust him (Psalm 147.11).
V. When we thank him (1 Thessalonians 5:18).
VI. When we know more about the Lord Jesus (2 Peter 3:18).
VII. When we faithfully attend church meetings (Hebrews 10:25).

Other ways to honour God will become evident when you read the Bible. Don't ever let circumstances or the devil bombard you with negative thoughts about yourself or about your salvation. You are a child of the King.

Chapter Seven
Grace to Help in Times of Need

I quite like the way Thomas Aquinas described grace. Aquinas was a 13th Century Catholic Priest and an Italian Dominican Friar, Theologian and Philosopher. What really attracted me to him is the fact that he was the foremost classical proponent and indeed the father of Natural Theology, a branch of study that provides arguments for the existence of God based on reason and ordinary experience of nature.

Aquinas described grace as 'the assistance of God', 'Auxilium Dei'. It is only by the assistance which God provides that we can navigate through especially during periods of great stress and need. In a world of noise, confusion, and relentless pressures, people long for peace of mind and calmness. True peace of heart and mind is only available to us through faith in Jesus Christ.

Grace is God's free gift to His beloved. It is His ability imparted unto us. Grace is strength and courage when we are weak, and or feel used and abused. Grace is that power that comes to us to enable us to live a peaceful life amid chaos and the continuing madness around us today. Grace is the work of God and only He can understand it, it is unsearchable and amazing. Grace helps us smile even when there are bills to be paid or when we receive a not-so-good report from hospital. During such moments, we definitely need the assistance of God, as Thomas Aquinas argued. It was as if he had in mind what the apostle Paul says in 1 Corinthians 1:4

"I thank my God always concerning you for the grace of God which was given to you by Christ Jesus."

They were strengthened by spiritual gifts so that they may remain blameless and faithful on the day of our Lord Jesus Christ.

I assure you, no matter what you are going through right now, there is grace from the throne room to take you to the other side of victory! Believe me, sometimes suffering is the training ground for Christian maturity. There is grace all the way.

Grace, I'm sure you remember, means 'unmerited favour and mercy of God', but on a deeper sense there are two types of grace, that I have identified according to the scriptures. Common Grace is the type of grace which leads to saving grace and I believe everyone on earth is permitted to receive this, because the Bible says,

"For God so loved the world that He gave His only begotten Son, that whoever believes in Him should not perish but have everlasting life." John 3:16

God loves the world, not the church and He gave His only begotten Son Jesus Christ so that anyone who believes should not perish, not anyone who belongs to the Church. Saving grace is available to all. We deserve hell, but God by His grace gives us redemption. It is balm for the broken. The second one is called Special Grace which leads to living grace. The common grace is experienced by all irrespective of belief, creed, or relationship with Christ. We know that the sun shines for everyone and it rains on everyone. Everyone on earth is entitled to family, food, health, employment and so on.

"That you may be sons of your Father in heaven; for He makes His sun rise on the evil and on the good and sends rain on the just and on the unjust." Matthew 5:45

But Special Grace is what the believer in Christ experiences which enables them to run the race. There are two Greek words which the English Language uses to describe the word 'race'. One is *stadion* which looks like the contest in the Greek games and our 200 metres dash in the Olympics. The other one is *argon* – the struggle or battle which someone has with themselves, the internal daily struggles and conflicts required to make us conform to the image of Christ. Special grace is the divine life, power and ability of God flowing and operating through a believer to give us supernatural power and ability for ministry and sanctification. My worry is that most people in the Church stop at the experience of saving grace and sit on the pew as 'receivers' for donkey years. Christian experience is not a 'spectator sport', we must be participators in the Kingdom! When you are a spectator, you don't go ahead to accomplish what you are 'graced' for. Every believer has a living grace to accomplish something for The Master. Pastors, evangelists, Sunday school teachers, class teachers, prayer warriors, singers/musicians and so on, or as marketplace ministers – nurses, traders, carers, doctors, IT specialists, etc. I don't believe that there is a Christian without a spiritual gift!

"And He Himself gave some to be apostles, some prophets, some evangelists, and some pastors and teachers, for the equipping of the saints for the work of ministry, for the edifying of the body of Christ, till we all come to the unity of the faith and of the knowledge of the Son of God, to a perfect man, to the measure of the stature of the fullness of Christ; that we should no longer be children, tossed to and fro and carried about with every wind of doctrine, by the trickery of men, in the cunning craftiness of deceitful plotting," Ephesians 4:11-14

When Jesus spoke to His disciples, and the believers of today by extension. I believe it was to encourage them and comfort them on things that were to come.

"These things I have spoken to you so that in Me you may have peace. In the world you will have tribulation; but be of good cheer. I have overcome the world." John 16:33

The grace of God is essentially everything that God has made available to the believer. The grace of God is routed through many systems that we are familiar with. It comes in the form of mercy, spiritual gifts, the fruit of the Spirit, prosperity, and many other ways that God uses as advantages for the believer here on earth.

The system of God's grace provides exactly what the believer needs at the exact point of need. It is true that God works in His own time, but we are also in sync with His will and this grace can keep us until that hour of His salvation.

"Seeing then that we have a great High Priest who has passed through the heavens, Jesus the Son of God, let us hold fast our confession. For we do not have a High Priest who cannot sympathize with our weaknesses, but was in all points tempted as we are, yet without sin. Let us therefore come boldly to the throne of grace, that we may obtain mercy and find grace to help in time of need." Hebrews 4:14-16

What Grace Can Do

God's grace is the unmerited gift that He gives to people. Grace has many manifestations, and principally, anything that is released from God can be termed "the grace of God". Grace has nothing to do with what we can do, but when it comes upon us, we are enabled to do far beyond the natural capacity that should have limited us.

Paul says about the grace of God in helping him achieve so much in the work of God:

"But by the grace of God I am what I am, and His grace toward me was not in vain; but I laboured more abundantly than they all, yet not I, but the grace of God which was with me." 1 Corinthians 15:10

He excitedly talks of the grace of God that must have helped him in his many times of need. Paul had times of need; from material needs to spiritual needs. He was a man that was mightily helped by the grace of God, and he didn't hide this.

The grace of God is the provision of God in the time of your need without which, there is nothing for faith to receive. So, it is by faith that we receive what the grace of God has released to us. The salvation that we have received is grace. This was a form of need that God satisfied which was the need for mankind to be saved. But how did the salvation come? Through the grace of God:

"Through whom also we have access by faith into this grace in which we stand and rejoice in the hope of the glory of God."
Romans 5:2

The grace of God manifests in all the areas of our lives where we need help. And like I have told you before now, the grace of God is not limited to only your spiritual salvation, but God is also releasing His grace into everything that concerns you. Here is what Peter says in his letter:

"As His divine power has given to us all things that pertain to life and godliness, through the knowledge of Him who has called us by glory and virtue" 2 Peter 1:3

This is the grace of God to us. He says, *"Has given us all things that pertain to life",* this is not talking about spiritual life, because right there he says, *"and godliness",* which now suggests the spiritual life. God has made all grace abound toward you, and all you must do is to ask and receive.

When the bible says, 'all grace', it does not exclude any aspect of your life. God gives this grace so that we can do every good work that we are supposed to partake in.

"And God is able to make all grace abound toward you, that you, always having all sufficiency in all things, may have an abundance for every good work" 2 Corinthians 9:8

So, whatever your need may be, all it takes is asking your heavenly Father for the grace to provide a solution for your need.

Where to Find Grace

Though there is grace readily available to the believer as part of God's kindness, there is still an obtaining of that grace. You need to know how to engage this grace in your life, so you don't suffer lack where God has already provided for you. Grace is found in God. He is the Father of all grace, which means that He is the Father of every good thing, since we affirm that His grace is everything good that comes from Him:

"But may the God of all grace, who called us to His eternal glory by Christ Jesus, after you have suffered a while, perfect, establish, strengthen, and settle you." 1 Peter 5:10

God is the Father of every good thing. How can He not want to give you the good things that He possesses? The bible states this as a fact:

"Every good gift and every perfect gift is from above and comes down from the Father of lights, with whom there is no variation or shadow of turning." James 1:17

The grace of God is found in God. When you have a need, it is important that you know whom you serve, so that you know what is obtainable and what is not. The Bible says that the throne of God is where abundance of grace is found, and this grace manifests as mercy and other dimensions that answer our needs. Hallelujah!

"Let us therefore come boldly to the throne of grace, that we may obtain mercy and find grace to help in time of need." Hebrews 4:16

If we do not come to God through the instrument of prayer in a time of need, then we may miss out on the help that is readily available in Him. The verse above is talking about coming to God through fervent prayer. The place of prayer for a believer carries an immeasurable weight of advantage that cannot be overemphasized. If you must enforce the victory of Christ in your journey of life and faith as a believer, then prayer is something you cannot do without.

The Bible teaches us to pray so much. Jesus taught us to pray, the apostles continued this tradition and taught us to do the same as well. Prayer is communicating with God. it is the place where we lay bare our all before God, showing Him our inadequacies and asking for His help to empower us. We are encouraged to pray consistently as spiritual people:

"Pray without ceasing." 1 Thessalonians 5:17

There are no conditions to praying; it is for all seasons. When we are having it good, we must pray; and when things are rough and falling apart, prayers must continue. (Philippians 4:6).

We must pray in the spirit and in the understanding that we have. Praying in the spirit is powerful. In fact, in the book to the Corinthians, it says:

"What is the conclusion then? I will pray with the spirit, and I will also pray with the understanding. I will sing with the spirit, and I will also sing with the understanding." 1 Corinthians 14:15

"But you, beloved, building yourselves up on your most holy faith, praying in the Holy Spirit," -Jude 20

"And take the helmet of salvation, and the sword of the Spirit, which is the word of God; praying always with all prayer and supplication in the Spirit, being watchful to this end with all perseverance and supplication for all the saints." Ephesians 6:18

Praying in the Spirit involves using the sword of the Spirit. This is called praying with spirit-led scriptures. The sword of the Spirit is the 'rhema' word of God. Praying in the Spirit also connotes praying seriously and consistently for other believers, that is, intercession, because the apostle Paul flows from 'praying in the Spirit' to 'praying for the saints' in the same verse of scripture. Intercession for the saints is a cardinal work of the Holy Spirit.

Praying in the Spirit also means praying with the Spirit's miscellaneous influence. The deeper our relationship with God, the more we will have spirit-guided feelings, impressions, urges, images, thoughts, intentions, and resolves when we pray. This is what releases the grace that God gives us. Prayer must be paramount to a believer's walk. With the understanding of the word of God, there is greater power released in the place of prayer.

Pray as the Spirit leads you, even if you are not speaking in terms you understand, sometimes it is the move of the Spirit to make you pray for even what you are not aware of. The bible says:

"He who speaks in a tongue edifies himself..." 1 Corinthians 14:4

The Spirit helps us to pray in order that these graces that we need when we are helpless will come to us for our help and salvation. (Romans 8:26).

Chapter Eight
Living Faithfully in A Compromised World

Faithfulness is an essential characteristic that God looks for in the lives of those who follow him. Our righteousness is in Christ, and we are in the world but not of the world. The Bible records many examples of men and women who lived in perfect faithfulness to God and were rewarded for it, like Moses, who was *"faithful in all the house of God"* (Hebrews 3:5).

Many people find it challenging to live faithfully with God because of all the temptations in this world. We must resist the influence of the world by making a firm resolve to live out our beliefs, and when we brand ourselves as Christians, we are kept from the compromise that comes from mingling with the world and its pressures. God is faithful, our temptations will not exceed our strength, and He has planned the way out for us.

"No temptation has overtaken you except such as is common to man; but God is faithful, who will not allow you to be tempted beyond what you are able, but with the temptation will also make the way of escape, that you may be able to bear it." 1 Corinthians 10:13

What do you need to do?

Be grateful

A faithful man or woman has a grateful heart and accepts everything with thanksgiving. Let's learn to say thank you to God and show gratitude to all the people who help us move forward in faith. We overcome the enemy with a thankful spirit and not a heart full of complains and regrets. Thanksgiving in a certain way is easy to do when the blessings are falling around your ears, but it can be very difficult to do when it seems that the trials are falling down around your ears, and still in those things, we are told to give thanks.

I was once told the story of Helen Keller. She was born in 1882, but when she was 19 months old, she was ravaged by a fever that left her without sight and without the ability to hear. She was locked in a world of darkness and silence; but she was determined and was extremely smart. Helen determined that she would be able to communicate with the outside world, so she began to imitate to her family things that she wanted. When she wanted a piece of bread, she would make a hand motion as if she were cutting a piece of bread to let her family know. When she wanted ice-cream, she would wrap her arms around herself, and she would shiver. She developed about sixty different motions that she could do to communicate with her family, but it frustrated her as she understood that people communicated with their lips, and she couldn't communicate with her lips to her family. And as she grew, she became more and more frustrated and more and more violent because of her frustration. She would smash things; she would throw objects. She was out of control. At age seven, her parents got her a tutor to help her learn to communicate. And very instrumental in Helen Keller's ability to cope with this was her trust in the living God. Later, in her life, Helen said this 'for three things I thank God every day of my life. Thanks that He has vouchsafed me knowledge of His works; deep thanks that He has set in my darkness the light of faith; deepest thanks that I have another life to look forward to – a life joyous with light and flowers and heavenly song.' Helen Keller may not have been thankful for the circumstances that God had dealt to her, but she was thankful in that circumstance.

"Rejoice always, pray without ceasing, in everything give thanks; for this is the will of God in Christ Jesus for you." 1 Thessalonians 5:16-18

How in the world can I do this? You don't understand my circumstances!

You are right, my friend, I don't understand the circumstances in which God has called you to give thanks. You don't have any idea how great a challenge it is to me to give thanks either. But the apostle tells us how, and it's here in just three words, 'in Christ Jesus.' It is only possible to express thanks to God in everything if you have a faith relationship with Jesus Christ – if you are in Christ. It is only in and through Jesus Christ that we can give thanks in every circumstance.

It was St. Augustine who once said, 'Lord command what You will, but give what You command.' I think he is saying 'Lord I can't do the things that you tell me to do, but You can command them and then You can give me the ability to do what You command.'
When you are connected to the One who is the spiritual source of the capacity to be thankful in every circumstance, then you'll be able to give thanks in everything. May God grant that we would be thankful people.

Be willing
The heart of man is sinful by nature. The first thing that God will require of us is a willing, humble heart, ready to love and obey him. We must make a conscious effort to do this because it does not come by itself. You must decide daily to present yourself worthy unto Him and ask that He will make your heart to be like Him. There are days when you might not really feel like going on, but the Lord looks out for your willing heart.

"But the natural man does not receive the things of the Spirit of God, for they are foolishness to him; nor can he know them, because they are spiritually discerned." 1 Corinthians 2:14

Be committed

When God calls us, He certainly desires an answer, but not only that. He also expects us to prove our love to Him by surrendering ourselves completely, as Jesus did. Our level of zeal and fruitfulness will depend on the degree of our commitment. There are many gullible people inside the Church today, they are shallow and devoid of strong commitment and little wonder why firebrand faith is in the decline. Living faithfully for Jesus in a post-modern era demands a very firm commitment and a strong resolve to be completely sold out to Jesus. We live in a day and age when evangelical Christianity is constantly under attack, even from fellow Christians. Truth is that sometimes, standing with the authority of the scriptures would feel like going against the flow, but I am aware that Christianity itself, as we have said repeatedly, is counter cultural. Changing world, yes, but we are handed down an unchanging Word. We don't need to water down our commitment for Jesus because we are interested in impressing our comrades who are battling with some strongholds, we should be full of love, that's what Jesus would do. He loves us even as dirty as we are. What He doesn't love, we've been told, is our sins. He wants us delivered and clean. We are all unworthy but through His blood He has redeemed us and made us worthy, hallelujah!

"Commit your works to the LORD, and your thoughts will be established." Proverb 16:3

Be obedient

Getting involved is not everything. King Saul went up as instructed but did not follow the full instructions given to him (1 Samuel 15:15). To be faithful is to follow the roadmap that God gives us to the letter to "fight according to the rules" (2 Timothy 2: 5). There are no shortcuts to take, no compromises. We can't negotiable our way out of the will of God, we must submit to it completely. Every good builder builds according to the rules else the whole project comes crashing down in due course. Our allegiance must be to the risen Lord who has no hidden shadow or darkness and is never subject to change. His word is settled in heaven.

"And also, if anyone competes in athletics, he is not crowned unless he competes according to the rules." 2 Timothy 2:5

Request for God's guidance

Whatever field of action we wish to undertake, we must adopt an effective strategy to have results. It is the Holy Spirit who gives it to us. Prayer and meditation on the Word are the means by which God guides us. We receive divine strategy from the Lord and the Holy spirit guides us into all truth which helps us to dismantle the traps of the enemy. He is ever ready to lend a helping hand if we will ask Him.

Trust in God totally

Although intelligence and human strength are essential in the service to God, it is also necessary to know how to make room for the supernatural. Today we see too many human schemes, agenda and programme and not enough reliance on the leadership and inspiration of the Holy Spirit, no wonder the body of Christ struggles. We are often limited, but God is not. This is why faith must be stimulated through the miracles and the power of God. He can lift us up from the gutter-most to the uttermost and see us transformed and live a new life that pleases Him where it will be simply natural to live in the supernatural.

"Casting all your care upon Him, for He cares for you." 1 Peter 5:7

Be patient

Being patient and knowing how to wait is also a proof of loyalty. Unfortunately, we are often impatient and therefore miss out on the blessing! A faithful heart knows how to patiently wait for God's promises, however long it may take. King Saul received God's instructions through Prophet Samuel, as I mentioned above, but partly because of impatience, (and greed of course) he deviated from what he was told to do and showed no loyalty at all. The result? He was summarily rejected by the Lord as king, and David was chosen instead.

"And let us not grow weary while doing good, for in due season we shall reap if we do not lose heart." Galatians 6:9

Be disciplined

There is no loyalty without increased discipline and vigilance. God has not given us a spirit of fear, but of power and of love and of a 'well-disciplined mind.' This discipline has come from the Greek word *'sophronismos,'* it could also be seen as 'a sound mind.' When you have a faithful heart, you will adopt the right behaviour, watching over yourself. Assessing yourself always and making the necessary adjustment. It is crucial to have a personal discipline in our spiritual life if we must live inside out in an upside-down world.

Be productive

God expects his children to be productive. He has given us a field and is waiting to reap the fruits of it. A job done with delay and carelessness testifies to a lukewarm heart. Even when it seems that we are making no headway, we must continue and persevere in the task. God wants us to be productive in our world. Do you remember the parable that Jesus told the people who put a testing question across to Him in Luke chapter 13? The Lord Jesus said there was a man who planted a fig tree in his orchard. But every time he came to gather fruit from his tree, he found none, for it was barren, so he said to his gardener, 'For the last three years I've come to gather figs from my tree, but it remains fruitless. What a waste! Go ahead and cut it down!' But the gardener protested, 'Sir, we should leave it one more year. Let me fertilize and cultivate it, then let's see if it will produce fruit. If it doesn't bear figs by next year, we'll cut it down.' Our challenge is that we don't need to wait until the future to be productive, because He has bestowed on us absolutely everything necessary for a dynamic spiritual life and godliness,
through true and personal knowledge of Him who called us by His own glory and excellence. The rest lies on us. We have no excuse for failure.

Be accountable

As we accept Christ into our lives, we must be accountable to Him for our activities, whether family, social, or spiritual. Being accountable to God for everything we do allows us to remain humble and dependent on Him.

"So then each of us shall give account of himself to God."
Romans 14:12

God is always with us when things are good and when they are not so good. We, too, must learn to remain faithful, for it is then that God will recognize in us a pure and sincere desire to serve and belong to Him until the end of our life. As Christians, we know we will face oppositions and be rejected even as Christ was. But just as the Father sent him into the world, He has sent us also (John 17:14-15), with the assurance that He is with us every day.

"Teaching them to observe all things that I have commanded you; and lo, I am with you always, even to the end of the age. Amen."
Matthew 28:20

The Christian life is a daily struggle. We fight against the sin that fights inside us. We are called to put to death our mortal bodies. Our hearts are crooked (Jeremiah 17:9-10), unfathomable (1 Corinthians 4.3-5) and deceptive. Every day we should ask God to search us to help us discern the sin within us (Psalm 139.23-24). Through the Word, the Holy Spirit reveals our sins to us. But we must beware of two traps; morbid introspection and focusing on one sin to the detriment of everything else. God does not let us fight sin on our own, but we rely on the grace and power of God (Colossians 1:11).

"That He would grant you, according to the riches of His glory, to be strengthened with might through His Spirit in the inner man," Ephesians 3:16

Chapter Nine
Step Out in Faith

If we spend all the time complaining about our misery or failure, sickness, or even our family situation or disadvantaged background, nothing will change. What makes the change is that we put our faith to practice, no matter how small we think there is, our faith can surprise us and work wonders. In fact, we have seen through the accounts of Jesus' dealing with people during His earthly ministry that miracles only happen when we make a move. I want you to know that God has promised to take us step by step by step; not all at once but step by step, and each step will be a miracle, so you need faith to unlock the miracle. He is a God of plan, purpose, and design.

God's miracle-working power will be released within your life as you make up your mind that regardless of the circumstances or problems you face, you are not going to stay where you are, but you are going to get up and go forward, acting in faith upon God's word until you receive whatever you are believing and asking Him for.

Naaman the leprous Army General in 2 Kings 5, did not receive his miracle of healing until he got up from where he was and acted upon the word of the Lord spoken through Prophet Elisha, the man of God. Most times, we, like Naaman will prefer to remain as we are because of pride and being simply conceited. General Naaman was described as a very courageous person, but this quality did not get him anywhere near his miracle until he stepped out in faith.

We can also learn a lesson from the four lepers sitting outside the walls of Samaria.

"Now there were four leprous men at the entrance of the gate; and they said to one another, "Why are we sitting here until we die? If we say, 'We will enter the city,' the famine is in the city, and we shall die there. And if we sit here, we die also. Now therefore, come, let us surrender to the army of the Syrians. If they keep us alive, we shall live; and if they kill us, we shall only die." 2 Kings 7:3,4

They didn't receive their miracle until they decided to get up and step out in faith and march forward. Many people cannot receive any breakthrough in life simply because they just wouldn't take risks, and indeed some people don't take risks for fear of failure. How can you be so sure? The only barrier between you and the thing you are believing for could be a step of faith. When you want what you don't have, you've got to risk doing what you haven't done yet.

The widow woman in the city of Zarephath with the cruse of oil and barrel of meal which did not dry up during the three and half years of famine did not receive the change she needed until she decided to get up from where she was and stepped out in faith upon the word of the Lord from Elijah the Tishbite. In her desperation she decided that the best thing to do would be to put her faith in action. (See 1 Kings 17:1-16)
While Jesus was on his way to Jerusalem, He was met with ten men who needed a divine touch. It might be that they expected Jesus to heal them by touching them, but He decided to give them a rather strange instruction.

"So, when He saw them, He said to them, "Go, show yourselves to the priests." And so it was that as they went, they were cleansed." Luke 17:14

They were healed 'as they went.' Their needs were met when they stepped out in faith and acted on the words of Jesus.

The woman who was suffering from a haemorrhage had this situation for twelve years, and not only that, she had spent all that she had paying for hospital bills and was not helped at all, but instead had become worse. But when she made up her mind to stop feeling pity for herself and stepped out from her house and out of her comfort zone, she pushed her way through the crowd and acted in faith and she received her divine healing. (Mark 5:25-34)

Simon Peter and his partners had fished all night without any catch in Luke chapter 5. Peter told Jesus,

> *'Master, we have toiled all night and have taken nothing;*
> *nevertheless, at your word, I will let down the net.'*

Nothing happened for them until they stepped out in faith and acted on the command of Jesus to launch out into the deep waters.

Beloved, I want you to know that regardless of the circumstances you are facing, and regardless how long you may have waited, regardless of how long you may have been praying and believing God to supernaturally intervene, you must be willing to say to the Lord, 'nevertheless, at your word I will act, I will step out, I will obey your word.' There must be a willingness, then an action on your path.

Faith requires sacrifice. A life of faith is a life of surrender. That faith demands total life on the altar. The fact is that without faith, it is impossible to please God. When it comes to faith, many people even question and criticize the way we use it and teach people how to use it. Truth remains that without faith, it is impossible to please God, and it is through faith that we come to Him. Now, what strikes me is God's willingness to honour those who use that tool, that power.

Once, two blind men followed the Lord Jesus, crying out for a cure.

"And when He had come into the house, the blind men came to Him. And Jesus said to them, "Do you believe that I am able to do this? "They said to Him, "Yes, Lord." Then He touched their eyes, saying, "According to your faith let it be to you." Matthew 9:28-29

Here's the thing; there is no resistance from God when a pure, bold, and robust faith is manifested. The Lord is always encouraged by our firm faith and commitment to His instructions. It was as if the Lord Jesus wanted to make sure of their willingness to step out of doubt and into the realm of receiving before He issued the command for healing.

God gives the best to those who choose Him as GOD of their lives. He did that through His Son, the Lord Jesus, when He delivered Him as the perfect sacrifice for humanity. And so, it is in the lives of those who lay their lives on His altar. They receive the best because they prioritize His will in their lives and, thus, He responds according to your faith.

Stepping out in faith means trusting God in whatever situation that you meet yourself. It means trusting God even when staying in the dark over a situation and at the same time believing that God will do something on your behalf because He is always with you.

Now, faith is the substance of things hoped for, the evidence of things not seen. Christians confidently trust God and follow up on His promises and the guarantee of His word. It is a substance or reality, even though we have not yet seen it, since God is consistent with His promises and cannot lie. Confidence is frequently misconstrued, and a few groups have instructed that you can meet your own cravings by asserting it through confidence. A few years prior, it was normal practice to hear devotees asserting what had a place with others and wanting to get it by confidence. In our world today, numerous individuals have more confidence in themselves and the world than confidence in God. This is in sharp differentiation to what exactly won in the Garden of Eden before the fall of Adam. Around then, Adam trusted and completely relied upon God. This changed when Adam decided to submit to the devil as opposed to God. Rather than conviction and reliance on God, he picked unbelief and autonomy from God. Confidence in God is the pathway back to God and venturing out in confidence is to re-establish our conviction and reliance on God.

Abram, before he was called Abraham, ventured out in confidence when God called him to leave his home in Ur of the Chaldees. Abram had a place with a rich group of icon admirers when God called him. God advised him to leave everything and everybody and go to a spot that He, God, would show him. There God advised him,

"I will make you an extraordinary country; I will favour you and make your name incredible, and you will be a gift." Gen. 12:20

Abram didn't have a clue where he was going; however, he trusted God and ventured out in confidence in dutifulness to God's Word. The call of God will consistently require a detachment as in Abram's situation, it was a partition from his family and previous existence. Abram obeyed yet not totally. He took his dad Terah and his nephew Lot with him. It was solely after the demise of his dad Terah and division from his nephew Lot that Abram had the full manifestation of the divine promise to go into the guaranteed endowments. Abraham grew in confidence till he trusted God totally and yielded each aspect of his life to Him in complete compliance. As of now, he was prepared to comply with God and offer up his hotly anticipated and adored child Isaac as an oblation to God.

There was a particular period in the ministry of Jesus when He received a request from a Canaanite woman to heal her daughter who was cruelly possessed by a demon. The word of the Lord tells us,

"But He answered her not a word. And His disciples came and urged Him, saying, "Send her away, for she cries out after us."²⁴ But He answered and said, "I was not sent except to the lost sheep of the house of Israel."²⁵ Then she came and worshiped Him, saying, "Lord, help me!"²⁶ But He answered and said, "It is not good to take the children's bread and throw it to the little dogs." Matthew 15:23-26

As we can see, this woman had to face some resistance and opposition from the disciples, and Jesus had to reiterate His specific commission. He said,

"I was commissioned by God and sent only to the lost sheep of the house of Israel."

She is commended for her doggedness which is a proof of her determination in response to the words of the Lord Jesus: "it is not right to take the children's bread and throw it to the dogs." There were several obstacles that day, but she was ready to successfully vanquish all.

We must bear in mind that many people before us have prevailed during trying and difficult times. The people of Israel were tested in the desert. David was too, and Abraham was tried by walking to Moriah to deliver his son Isaac; the Syrophoenician woman was being tested. When we pass through trials and times of silence, it is our faith in God that sustains and encourages us. It is important to note that the Lord Jesus had already said: "I am not sent but to the lost sheep of the house of Israel," but verse 21 tells us that the Lord went to the land of Tyre and Sidon (Phoenician cities, not the land of Israel), so there was a profound lesson from the Master for all the people who followed him and who believed in him.

This event also reminds us that when someone believes in the Lord Jesus and perseveres, they will see the supernatural and the powerful hand of the Lord on their behalf irrespective of their ethnicity and background. Nothing can stop them because God is faithful.

Here me again, there is no amount of challenge you are going through that has never happened to anyone before you, both in the present age and in the scriptures. We know that challenges are helpers of faith which helps build us as Christians, God uses them to test your faith in Him. Furthermore, if we check the life of Job, we could see that he passed through a lot of challenges during his time, but in the end, all he could say was,

"For I know that my Redeemer lives, And He shall stand at last on the earth;" Job 19:25

As a Christian, I want you to know that you may have tribulations, but as the scripture tells us you must be of good cheer because He has overcome the world. God is still God, and He still performs His promises. He listens to anyone who dares to step out in faith and believe in Him; He has never failed once, and He will not start with you. Hold on tight to Him, meditate on His word and keep calm to hear from Him; He will never forsake you.

Chapter Ten
Boldness and Courage in Times of Conflict

In our world today, inequality is soaring. The world is increasingly evil and dangerous. The more the day pass by, the more we hear of many abnormalities and inequalities. Social injustice and a continuing sense of the wide gap in the distribution of wealth stares us in the face. These have become apparent in the last few fears.

At every turn, there is possibly something to make you scream and be thrown into a well of thoughts about the kind of world we live in, and the miracle needed to survive every day. There is always something new in the news about the wickedness of this world. It is no wonder the word of God already announced the verdict on the hearts of people, when it said:

"The heart is deceitful above all things, and desperately wicked; who can know it?" Jeremiah 17:9

One of the biggest problems the world is facing is the problem of conflicts, which most times involves violence. Safety has become a very costly commodity. This is a very big issue these days, and the security of citizens is constantly threatened. There is hardly any week when we don't hear of conflicts both around us and further afield.

Just as the Bible rightly prophesied, nations have already started rising against nations. (Matthew 24:7). Even within nations, people have risen against each other to cause unrest and disaster. If you are not basing your protection upon something firm, you might just be the next victim. For evil men have risen to cause havoc, and who shall rescue the simple?

There is need to have boldness and courage in times like this, but this cannot be a vague claim that is not based on anything. There must be something or someone who can be a foundation to your claims.

Is there a solution?

The simple answer is yes. Will the solution last? That is a question for another day.

There are various solutions that we can proffer in the area of protection. Technology has rapidly enhanced things today. We have fighter jets, sophisticated weapons, and many inventions yet to be revealed, but are they a solution to lasting protection? The Bible tells us that some trust in horses and in chariots, but there are also those who trust in the Living God:

> *"Some trust in chariots, and some in horses; but we will remember the name of the LORD our God."* - Psalms 20:7

Who do you trust in? Chariots and horses here mean the things that we can see; the time-tested schemes and machinations which have been deemed powerful over time. Many of them by reason of use and experience. But the revelation in this passage is that even those things can still fail. There is nothing greater than the one who created those things, and that is God the Almighty. Trust in God and remember Him if you want to overcome the challenges of insecurity that plague the world. Don't rely on your own knowledge and certainly your intellect and abilities are insecure in themselves alone. He is the one who gives you the ability to be creative and successful.

Faith in God

Boldness comes from oneness with the One who has made all things, and who has all the power to do all things. It is unwise to boast of your abilities without the Holy One. Some people can exhibit some courage, but a closer look might prove they were just filled with Dutch courage because they cannot give you real protection and the courage that comes with it. Believers in Christ move in such real boldness unseen and unheard of anywhere else, which is a wonder to the person who lives in the flesh. We have the creator of the whole universe on our team.

God is All-powerful. He is to be compared to none. The bible says:

> *"God has spoken once; twice I have heard this, that power belongs to God."* Psalms 62:11

If you seek true protection and boldness, it cannot be found anywhere else other than in God Himself. The One who lives in you has never lost a battle before. He made the world, and men, so what could possibly catch Him unawares?

You need to know who the God you serve is, for you to obtain the confidence that is required to walk without fear on this earth. When you know the personality of God; that He has made all that we see by the words of His mouth and sits above the earth in the heavens where His throne is, you will be bold. Knowing that He watches the affairs of people and pronounces His judgment on the unrighteous, you will be encouraged and strengthened in your faith to trust Him more. When you know that life and death are in His hands, you will have the courage to speak life over yourself and your family, knowing that He said He will never leave you nor forsake you. Don't speak fear or talk based on your physical space, always look beyond, and see what power lies at your disposal in the spirit realm and you will soar above life's circumstances.

Having faith in God is the principal element to walking in exploits above the insecurities that scare people.

God says in Isaiah 54:17:

" 'No weapon formed against you shall prosper; and every tongue which rises against you in judgment, you shall condemn. This is the heritage of the servants of the LORD, and their righteousness is from Me,' says the LORD."

You may be tempted to think that God was speaking about spiritual powers here, well that is included in the package of our full security, but this was about the physical aspect. When you read the whole chapter, you will find out that God was speaking about physical protection.

Just as He says many times all through scriptures that He will protect and keep them safe, all who trust in Him. He will keep them from the evil one. He simply promised you that you will triumph over oppositions.

When you don't know the word of God, it is easy to fear because you don't know what He has spoken. Did He promise to protect you or not? He is not only interested in giving you eternal life, but His salvation package is also all-inclusive. In fact, the Greek word for salvation is *"Sozo"*. It's root meaning goes beyond just the forgiveness of sins. According to Strong's Concordance, *Sozo* also carries the idea of being physically healed of diseases and to be delivered from your enemy. In the spiritual sense, that enemy is the devil and his demons. Salvation, then, must mean more than simply being saved to go to heaven when you die. To be biblically saved means there are also earthly effects on our lives today. When you are saved, not only are you free from the judgement and wrath of God, but this salvation also includes the ability to resist temptations to sin in a pursuit of Christlikeness, to be set free from demonic attacks and oppression, and to receive healing in our physical bodies. All through the Bible we see many passages which talks about God's promises as included in *sozo*. One of them has become my favourite during the global uncertainty which plagued our world.

"Bless the Lord, O my soul, and forget not all His benefits: Who forgives all your iniquities, who heals all your diseases, who redeems your life from destruction, who crowns you with lovingkindness and tender mercies." PSALM 103:2-4

And Isaiah prophesied about the messiah when he said, *"But He was wounded for our transgressions, He was bruised for our iniquities; The chastisement for our peace was upon Him, And by His stripes we are healed."* ISAIAH 53:5

So, we see clearly that God is interested in our physical and spiritual wellbeing. He is interested in the total person. We are not just waiting for when we will go to heaven and then everything will be okay. To be too heavenly conscious would be to be earthly useless. You need to know these things in order that your faith will be built, so you can receive the total promises made to you as part of redemption.

God is a protector, a shield, and a refuge. He saves the upright in heart; those who have the Lord Jesus living in them. Living by faith is the access key to the life that God has planned for you. His word says:

"My defence is of God, who saves the upright in heart." Psalms 7:10

God is a mighty defence for everyone who calls upon Him for salvation. He protects and safeguards His children. You should not fear the insecurities all around you, but have your heart fixed on God.

"The LORD is my rock and my fortress and my deliverer, my God, my rock, in whom I will trust, my shield, and the horn of my salvation, my stronghold." Psalms 18:2

Oh, how wonderful it is to know God! Your confidence will be built when you know more about His rhema word spoken to you. The psalmist understands and knows God so much, that he is bold enough to declare that:

"Yea, though I walk through the valley of the shadow of death, I will fear no evil, for you are with me; Your rod and Your staff, they comfort me." Psalms 23:4

Can you get to that level of confidence? It can only come through an experiential walk with God, knowing and understanding His ways through fellowship with Him.

Boldness through the Holy Spirit

God has given you the Holy Spirit, He is the one who will make you bold. He will endure you with power, love, and a sound mind. He does not come to make you fear anything – physically or spiritually. He is the power of God to cast out fear from your heart. You cannot be afraid of the dangers of this world, knowing that God Himself is in you. He takes away all your fears and infuses your heart with boldness and courage to take on life:

"For you did not receive the spirit of bondage again to fear, but you have received the Spirit of adoption by whom we cry, 'Abba, Father.'" Romans 8:15

It is the Holy Spirit that makes you bold and confident because you know within you that you are of God. Therefore, if you are of God, then you are His child, and He will always listen to you when you call. He will protect you from every evil that comes against you. You are unstoppable and unconquerable because you carry divinity inside of you.

Chapter Eleven
Stay Strong

A fundamental purpose of life on earth is personal advancement and achievement. Therefore, there must be times of testing and dilemmas to create the opportunity for that development. Who hasn't had the need to be reassured in times of insecurity and testing? Who is so sure of themselves that they never wanted to have a stable influence in life? What child could become self-reliant if all important decisions were made by parents? The same is true of our Heavenly Father. He did not promise us a problem-free ride and definitely did not create us, so we don't face challenges and even difficulties as we have to make important decisions for us to progress, develop and succeed in this mortal probation. Happily, in His perfect love, He has provided us with a way to solve those problems as we grow in strength and ability. I mean the sustaining power of faith in times of uncertainty and trials and even dilemmas.

I will never forget the time in my life and personal journey when I was faced with very many trials and troubles and the Lord gently spoke the words of Proverbs 24:10 to me and this passage hit me like a flash and has stayed with me ever since.

"If you faint in the day of adversity, your strength is small."

Listen, God is interested in your welfare, His will is that through His abundant grace you will be made strong and perfect. After you have suffered for a little while, the God of all grace who imparts His blessings and favour who called you to His own eternal glory in Christ, will Himself complete, confirm, strengthen, and establish you making you what you ought to be. Receive His grace right now!

" But may the God of all grace, who called us to His eternal glory by Christ Jesus, after you have suffered a while, perfect, establish, strengthen, and settle you." 1 Peter 5:10

God has given us the ability to exercise faith so that we can find peace, joy, and purpose in life. However, to use that power, you must find faith in something. There is no stronger foundation than faith in Heavenly Father's love for you, faith in His plan for happiness, and faith in the ability and willingness of our Saviour Jesus Christ to fulfil all His promises. A little challenge that I have noticed is that when we stay too long in a particular setback, and without any sign of hope, we are tempted to begin to doubt His ability to pull us out of the mess and this feeling may place a very huge wedge on the way of good reason. But the word of God does not lie, and Jesus is ever ready and willing to bring God's promises to pass on our behalf. No experience is a waste so hang on and stay strong. He will come through for you.

Some do not understand faith and therefore do not make the most of it. Others think that all discussion of religion and guidance that comes through strong faith has no logical basis. They might be true because logic and faith do not mix. I hear people often say that Christians are brainwashed people, well, they are saying this in a negative sense but there's a little truth in their claim because you cannot serve the Lord fruitfully if you analyse the Bible with head knowledge. And without faith living within us it would be impossible to please God. For we come to God in faith knowing that he is real and that he rewards the faith of those who passionately seek him. A work of faith is not a work of uncertainty but that of assurance and reliance on the eternal promises of the Almighty God. To believe God and His Word most times goes against common sense and feels like going against the status quo.

Faith is not an illusion or magic, but a power rooted in timeless principles. Are you among those who have exercised faith and believe that they have not achieved the expected benefit? If so, it is likely that you have not understood or followed the principles on which it is founded.

Despite the steadfastness of your faith, God will not always immediately reward you according to your desires, but He will respond with what, in His eternal plan, is best for you. He loves you so deeply and fully that because we are human, we fail to see this, sometimes because of the many troubles looking us in the face and because of human mistakes. In fact, if you knew the fullness of His plan, you would never ask for anything contrary to it, even if you were tempted to do so. Sincere faith provides understanding and strength to accept Heavenly Father's will when it differs from ours. We will accept His will with peace and security, confident that His infinite wisdom surpasses our ability to fully understand His plan, which is gradually unfolding.

"I alone know the plans I have for you, plans to bring you prosperity and not disaster, plans to bring about the future you hope for." Jeremiah 29:11 (GNT)

Believers should understand that faith is not just pushing a button and getting an answer. Many times, we are reminded that people who received great breakthroughs in life had to put up with times of crisis and times of testing from the Lord. The Lord declared, "I rebuke and punish everyone I love; So be zealous, and repent" Revelation 3:19

Always, when counselling young people, I make them know that a problem-free life is only an illusion. In fact, becoming a Christian does not shield you from the normal challenges of life, instead, you are enrolled in an eternal confrontation with the forces of evil, but praise God that the victory has already been assured beforehand, your only requirement is to stay faithful and strong. In my personal journey with the Lord, I've heard Him say to me that the only way out is through. He might not pull you out of the battle but might have decided that the best thing for you would be to go through it and come out stronger. He will never abandon you halfway but will surely provide every necessary assistance through the Holy Spirit and through His Word. At the other end of the road, you will become a wonder to the world, and you will give counsel and help to others who would fall into such issues in their journeys. Just make up your mind to stay strong and grab every knowledge and experience from whatever life has handed down to you. Be very watchful of what you say and how you behave during trying times, these will affect the duration of your wilderness experience and will either hasten your spiritual training days or cause you to linger in them. Christian maturity is reflected through what we say while under pressure. Only spiritual babes will curse their God when things fall out of control, you must resolve to stay calm and sturdy enough to be able to withstand.

The three Hebrew boys in Daniel chapter three were saved when they went through a fiery trial because they remained faithful even in the face of temptations. Because they were adamant that they were not going to budge, King Nebuchadnezzar was filled with fury, and his facial expression changed toward them. Then he gave a command that the furnace be heated seven times hotter than usual and instructed strong men in his army to tie up Shadrach, Meshach, and Abednego in their trousers, their coats, their turbans, and their other clothes and to throw them into the furnace of the blazing fire. Because the king's command was urgent and the furnace was extremely hot, the flame of the fire killed the men who carried them up, yet they were untouched by the flaming blaze. God took them through the 'fire school' and when they 'graduated', they were not only celebrated but they became a source of inspiration to others and has been throughout generations.

God uses your faith to shape your character. This is true no matter your age, location, or experience in life. Character is the manifestation of what you will become. A morally strong character is the result of having made the right choices during life's trials. Your faith will guide you to make those correct choices. What you do and what you think determines who you are and what you will become. Therefore, the choices you make must be inspired by the Lord. You must meditate, pray, and exercise faith to be willing to make choices that are consistent with the Master's teachings. Those choices are made through your faith in things that you believe in, and by acting accordingly, they will be confirmed. We have been given enough guidance to last us through a lifetime. The Bible is God's inspired word and is still very relevant and indeed inerrant. It is the manufacturers instruction book, but sad to say that most people on earth today are like folk who discard the instruction manual when they purchase a new gadget. The guidance through His word will strengthen your trust in the Heavenly Father and the Saviour Jesus Christ. Your faith will shape the strength of character that will be available to you in times of urgent need. The character we develop in times of great challenge or temptation, shows up afterwards. Character is patiently woven with threads of principle, doctrine, and obedience. The test of your faith produces patience. But His complete work may be patient, so that you may be perfect and complete, without missing anything. The foundation of character is integrity. The worthy character will strengthen your ability to respond obediently to the Spirit's leading. You will come to have a righteous character, which is more important than what you have, what you have learned over time, or what goals you have achieved, which will result in being trusted. A righteous character provides the foundation for spiritual strength. It allows you to correctly make difficult and very important decisions in times of trial, even when they seem overwhelming.

Our Father's plan is wonderful. The exercise of faith builds character. Strengthened character increases your ability to exercise faith; therefore, your confidence in conquering the trials of life increases, and the strengthening cycle continues; In other words, the more your character is fortified, the more the power of your faith will be fortified.

The saying that you get only what you paid for applies to spiritual rewards as well. You receive what you have paid for in obedience and in faith on the Lord Jesus Christ, and in the diligent application of the truth you have received. What you get is the shaping of your character, the advancement of your ability, and the successful accomplishment of your purpose here on earth: to progress by being tested.

No matter what happens, no matter how confused the world gets, you can always count on the sustaining power of faith. That will never change. God's perfect love will never change, His Gospel plan gives meaning to life and seals your redemption. His plan is not just for you to be tested here on earth but also for you to receive the progress that comes from making correct faith-inspired decisions that are possible by virtue of your obedience. Why worry about difficulties or uncertainties that you have no control over? Your righteous character increases the possibility that you will never have to suffer them. When problems and trials come, your faith will guide you to solutions. Your peace of mind, your conviction in answers to puzzling problems, and your ultimate joy depend on your trust in the Heavenly Father and His Son, Jesus Christ. Ultimately, what is right will prevail and cause you to receive blessings now, as you faithfully obey God's commandments.

Remember that an inexhaustible, continuous, and ever-present source of peace and comfort is at your fingertips. There is no doubt that your Heavenly Father loves you whatever your circumstance, no matter what your trials, temptations, or tribulations are. That certainty will never change.

I testify that faith in God and His guidance through the Holy Spirit will sustain you in an increasingly troubled world. I testify that applying these principles we have reviewed will help you to be worthy of keeping the fire of faith burning in times of uncertainty and crisis. You must remain strong in the Lord and stay determined.

Chapter Twelve
In Everything Give Thanks

"In everything give thanks; for this is the will of God in Christ Jesus for you" 1 Thessalonians 5:18

It is a very difficult thing for us to comprehend how we are supposed to give thanks during times of hardships and challenges. How could God ask us to do such a thing especially when we face disappointments, losses, or unbearable heartache? We could try when we are happy or feel blessed. But during hard times!

The misunderstanding comes in thinking we're supposed to give thanks "for" everything when God is leading us to give thanks "in" everything. We may struggle with this concept and indeed resist the idea when we think God is telling us to be thankful "for" the difficulties. We might miss what He is telling us to do, which is to be thankful despite the problems, to not let disappointments, failures, losses, and hurts keep us from being thankful to Him. We've been able to establish that hard times are part of life, so it is time to just move on ahead and to do what the Word says. The enemy should not keep us in one place trying to figure out what is happening. Any moment you lose is a time he stole.

During tumultuous times, God asks us to focus on Him and His faithfulness to us, rather than on our circumstances; to dwell on His promise to never leave or forsake us and to trust Him to help us in every situation we face in life. We serve a faithful and covenant-keeping God! Sometimes, the situation might look so awful that it seems the promise is falling in pieces, but I have learnt to hold onto Him and His Word. Take salvation as an example. Most times you don't just feel like you are saved when you pass through things, but truth is that you are saved. So, God's promise is not what you feel, but what you have.

Let us look at this Bible verse in some of the other translations that I love:

"In every situation [no matter what the circumstances] be thankful and continually give thanks to God; for this is the will of God for you in Christ Jesus." - AMP

"Be thankful in all circumstances. This is what God wants from you in your life in union with Christ Jesus." – GNT

"Thank God no matter what happens. This is the way God wants you who belong to Christ Jesus to live." - The Message

"Be thankful in all circumstances, for this is God's will for you who belong to Christ Jesus." – NLT
"And in the midst of everything be always giving thanks, for this is God's perfect plan for you in Christ Jesus." – TPT

Being thankful in everything starts with the small stuff of life, where we can be watchful for the everyday type of issues that trigger ungrateful attitudes, like losing a parking space, or being caught in traffic or having a household appliance break down—all little things that can throw our attitudes off course.

Recently our oven was broken. As I placed a call across to the electrician, I recognised the potential stress and inconvenience associated with not being able to bake or cook my fish and chips, and how it could affect our attitudes in a negative way, we kept attentive to the risk. As we considered whether it could be fixed or needed replacing, instead of focusing on what we didn't have at that moment, we thanked God for all the years we've had one that works.

Through the experience, we gained a renewed appreciation for having a working oven and good kitchen. The electrician looked at it and advised that having a completely new one would be more economical. With our new one, we give thanks to God on a daily basis for being able to cook even at midnight.

Appreciation is a motivation to do more. There is this feeling that we have when being appreciated, also you can attest that you might not like people who find it difficult to acknowledge kind gestures; people who never say thanks no matter what you do for them. If any opportunity shows up to help the ingrate, you may think twice. However, you would gladly look out for any opportunity to show kindness to a grateful soul. Anyone who cultivates the habit of expressing appreciation is destined to receive more favours.

There is something we can learn from the typical African culture, which looks like the old Biblical way of honouring kings. Courtesy demands that when you approach your king/ ruler, you must first pay some obeisance. This is common in the West African society. The only thing that differs is the mode of expressing the obeisance. In some communities you must kneel or bow down, in some places it is to prostrate; you completely lie down in front of the king, it could also be by standing ovation or by a military-salute. At times it could be by verbal expression of the majesty of the king or in any other form. All petition, complaint, request, grievances, and everything must wait; obeisance must come first. This enables you to secure the attention of the king and thereafter you can present your request, petition, report, or whatever message you have brought to the king. If you need the king's attention you must approach him with praises. Those who understand this simple secret will always have their needs met. They will always secure prompt attention of the king.

Our God is not just a king, He is the king of kings (Rev 1:5), He is not just a superior military officer, He is the Lord of hosts (Rev 17:14 & Psalm 46:7), the maker and sustainer of the whole universe, the giver of life. Even the air we breathe is by His authority. A man like David understood this and quickly wrote;

"Enter into His gates with thanksgiving,
And into His courts with praise.
Be thankful to Him and bless His name." Psalm 100:4

No wonder God called him "a man after my heart", a man that knows how to approach God. When we understand this, we will always approach God with thanks and praise.

We can choose to start each day by giving thanks to God IN our everyday circumstances.

"Giving thanks always for all things to God the Father in the name of our Lord Jesus Christ"- Ephesians 5:20

Thanksgiving builds up your faith. It is true that most times our present problems becloud our heart so much that we can hardly remember anything God has done for us in the past. However, no matter how big our present problem might be it is important to remember that there are some problems God has solved for us in the past. When you call to mind the past goodness and deliverances that you received, the past problems He had solved for you, the mercies He bestowed on you in the past, I mean when you appreciate God for past mercies, He lavished on you then you are invariably building up your faith thus: if He has done it in the past, He can do it again. If He has saved you in the past, He can save you again.

In the process of acknowledging His past help, you might eventually recall a past problem He solved for you, which was equally as big as the present one you are battling with. You might even discover that your present problem is not as enormous as certain problems solved in the past, hence your faith and trust is boosted, and trust rekindled. The same God who did it in the past can still do it again and as a result you see yourself coming out of depression into a state of hope and remain positive until you overcome.

To "give thanks in all things" implies both in good times and bad times. That includes when you face disappointment, in sickness, in want, bankruptcy, in hunger, in loss of job, loss of loved one, loss of property, even when betrayed by close confidants. In any and every situation you must give thanks. As a Christian you need to mature to a stage where thanksgiving becomes a habit and does not have to depend on pleasant situations or happy times; a level where you thank God for everything, literally. The disciples of Jesus Thanked God that they were counted worthy to suffer for Christ. During their suffering, they were grateful to God that they had the honour of suffering for Christ (James 1:2). This kind of thanksgiving can only come from a heart that has been redeemed by Jesus, a heart that is saved; a heart, which has been surrendered to Jesus Christ. So, the first step to take is to accept Jesus Christ as your Lord and personal saviour.

Thanksgiving is a weapon used in fighting spiritual battles. Those who understand this secret engage in thanksgiving when faced with life challenges. We can see Paul and Silas in Acts of the Apostles chapter 16 verses 25 -26 when they were imprisoned for preaching the gospel. They were not only imprisoned but they were chained even inside the prison. However, in their troubles they chose to be thankful. They sang praises to God. As they sang and praised God, their chains fell off and the doors of the prison opened on its own accord. The battle they could not fight for themselves was fought and won mysteriously while they were praising God.

Forms of thanksgiving

Thanksgiving can be in different forms. Let us look at some of them and see what lessons we could learn.

Singing
"Oh, sing to the Lord a new song!
For He has done marvellous things;
His right hand and His holy arm have gained Him the victory."
Psalm 98:1

The most common expression of thanksgiving is by singing praises to God. When you hear someone singing melodious praises the first thing that comes to your mind is that 'this fellow must be happy, something good must have happened to him'. There are several songs of praises one can sing to God in thanksgiving and praise. This form of thanksgiving is always readily available. It does not cost any money and you don't necessarily need someone to help you. You can do it anywhere any time. So next time you receive divine intervention in your life just raise one song of praise unto God.

As I mentioned before, David was a musician and when faced with difficulties, he praised his way out of despair. He praised his way out of discouragement. There are times when no one will encourage you, so you must learn to encourage yourself in the Lord through singing. Even when King Saul was tormented by an evil spirit, they called for David to sing and the spirit left Saul (1 Sam16:14-23, 2 Sam 22).

Testimony

Another form of thanksgiving is by testimony. That is by telling others what the Lord has done so that they thank God with you. You can also do thanksgiving for other people's testimonies.

Psalm 105:1-2 *"...make known among the nations what He has done... tell of His wonderful acts."* (NIV)

And like I told you earlier, this was one of the ways that David encouraged himself in the Lord. In 1 Samuel chapter 17 from verse 34 to 36, when he was ridiculed by Goliath, he remembered how God had helped him tear the lion and the bear that had come after the sheep he was taking care of. Maybe you should remind yourself of the good things God did for you or for others. Perhaps He had answered some prayers before? Thank Him for those things. You can also get encouragement from other people's testimonies. There is power in testimonies and proclaiming His goodness.

Offerings

Another way is by giving offering. That is by bringing money or other valuable materials into the treasury of the Lord. Psalm 107:22

let them present thanks-offering and loudly proclaim what the Lord has done" (NIV)

Lifting of hands

Another way of expressing thanksgiving is by lifting of hands or waving hands unto the Lord.

"Lift up your hands in the sanctuary and praise the Lord." Psalm 134:2

Some other forms of thanksgiving include but not limited to dancing, clapping of hands, use of musical instruments.

Psalm 47:1 *"Oh, clap your hands, all you peoples! Shout to God with the voice of triumph!"*

"Praise him with trumpets blasting! Praise him with piano and guitar! Praise him with drums and dancing! Praise him with loud clashing of cymbals! Praise him upon the high-sounding cymbals! Let everyone everywhere join in the crescendo of ecstatic praise to Yahweh! Hallelujah! Praise the Lord!" Psalm 150

Why we fail to give thanks

There are many factors that can hinder us from giving thanks. However, when we understand the importance of thanksgiving, we will not permit anything to hinder us.

Procrastination

It is important to know that our thanksgiving is to appreciate God and not to impress men. Procrastination, they say is the enemy of time. Why wait until when you think the cloud is favourable before you thank God? Let us thank Him when we feel like it and when we don't.

When the favour done to us seems to be small

A lot of times we tend to belittle God's favour. We take it for granted for example the breath in our nostrils may look common but, not everyone who wished to be alive today are alive. What we call common most times is not actually common. If you look well, you will discover that the mercy God has shown you is not shown to all who wanted it. You are selected and blessed. You may be waiting for God to raise the dead before you can thank Him, however, although God has all it takes to do the undoable, we must learn to praise Him for those things that seem little; therefore, He will be motivated to do greater things for us.

When we feel that we are qualified to receive the favours we received

You may have prayed and fasted before God answered you and did you that favour but believe me there are other people who equally fasted and prayed but did not receive.

"...the race is not to the swift, or the battle to the strong, nor does food come to the wise, or wealth to the brilliant, or favour to the learned; but time and chance happen to them all"

(Ecclesiastes 9:11)

You may have put in so much effort and worked so hard to achieve the feat you achieved but believe me there are other people who made the same preparation or even more but could not achieve. The difference is God's favour. If the Lord refuses to help you, you will remain helpless.

"Except the Lord Keeps a city the watchman stays awake in vain"
Psalm 127: 1-2

Therefore, for every achievement, for every success, for every blessing, for every deliverance, for every accomplishment, big or small, we must learn to give thanks.

Another factor that can hinder us from being thankful is when we receive less than we wanted. Even though you do not have all you need you are still alive and if there is life there is hope. But those who understand the need to be grateful will be grateful in all situations. For example, we know that statistics have shown that people from minority ethnic groups are likely to be paid far less than their counterparts from white background. This is according to some news report from BBC and other sources. But I have met people from BAME background who prays, "oh Lord, I thank you that you have not left me empty handed. Thank you that I can work and be entitled to my wages. I thank you because I know you have better plans for me to give me a better future, to take me higher than where I am now. I know that my future will be better than my today". A grateful person will surely be a great achiever no matter the little they have.

We read from the Bible that our Lord was grateful and full of thanks as He took the only available food which was far too less to feed the people. The power of thanksgiving, I believe, did the miracle. In the end the whole crowd of people ate thoroughly and had some left over. That is the power of gratitude.

"And he directed the people to sit down on the grass. Taking the five loaves and the two fish and looking up to heaven, he gave thanks and broke the loaves. Then he gave them to the disciples, and the disciples gave them to the people. They all ate and were satisfied, and the disciples picked up twelve basketfuls of broken pieces that were left over." Matthew 14:19-21

Another hindrance to thanksgiving is comparison

Believe me, when you are busy comparing yourself with other people you will hardly see anything worthwhile in yourself. You will only see misery and peril. How then can you be thankful when all you see about yourself is pity? The truth is that some of the people you envy are living a fake life. They may be showing off what they are not. They may be living on borrowing. It is very easy to mistake greed for ambition. Whereas healthy desires are good, but unnecessary unhealthy competition is bad. Be honest to yourself for once; why do you desire to be blessed? Is it to live a bogus flamboyant life? Is it to show off? Is it to be like others? It is usually greener on the other side of the field until you eventually cross over to the other side only to discover that it is not real pasture but artificial grass. However, if you want to be honest, even if God has not solved all your problems at least He has solved some. Why not appreciate him for the good times.

Let me conclude this chapter by advising that it is unwise to think that our success and achievements are because of our effort alone. He has given us His grace. Let us appreciate God for giving us grace and mercy. On the other hand, when things are not going well as you expected, learn to give thanks also because He who knows tomorrow is able to work through a seemingly bad situation and turn them around for good. An African adage says, "Tomorrow is pregnant."

Chapter Thirteen
It's Time to Dream Again

I believe the Lord has blessed you so far through the pages of this book and that you are encouraged to believe for the best and to get back your allotted inheritance. May I take you through one last journey.

Joseph was Rachel's firstborn and Jacob's eleventh son. You will agree with me that he must have been a very attractive and well-built bloke, the guy was a victim of the notorious wife of the Egyptian officer named Potiphar, we are told in Genesis 39:1-20 that Potiphar's wife who was known for her infidelities took a liking to Joseph and attempted to seduce him. When Joseph eluded these advances of this lady, she falsely accused him of having assaulted her, using the outer vestment which Joseph left in her hands when he ran for his dear life as evidence against Joseph.

Sometimes in our life, we pass through turbulent and trying times even when we believe we are in the right, does that strike a chord with you? During such moments, we may cry out "where are you Lord?" Have you ever received a prophetic word from God and rather than going smoothly, life brings temptations? You are not alone.

One of these days, the Lord gave me a very powerful word through the life experiences of Joseph.

> *"Until the time that his word came to pass,*
> *The word of the Lord tested him."* Psalm 105:19

Psalm 105 belong to the group of psalms called the historical psalms; they were vivid reminders of God's past acts on behalf of Israel. These history songs were written for passing on important lessons to succeeding generations. This psalm was sung as part of the celebration of David's bringing the ark of the covenant to Jerusalem. We see from the story of the Jewish people how consistently God's people failed to learn from the past. They repeatedly turned from fresh examples of God's faithfulness and forgiveness only to plunge back into sin.

It might be that Britain and indeed Europe is in this place right now. I belong to the school of thought that favours this study. The current decline and state of things in the Christian landscape remind us how often we do the same thing as the Jewish people. We have every reason to live for God, we choose instead to live for everything but God. If we paid more attention to "His story," we wouldn't make so many mistakes in our own stories. The land of the Wesleys and Whitefield has clearly lost it. Evan Roberts and the Welsh revivalists would regret their efforts if they were here. Shortly before he passed into glory in 1947, we are told that Smith Wigglesworth prophesied, *"During the next few decades there will be two distinct moves of the Holy Spirit across the church in Great Britain. The first move will affect every church that is open to receive it and will be characterized by the restoration of the baptism and gifts of the Holy Spirit. The second move of the Holy Spirit will result in people leaving historic churches and planting new churches. In the duration of each of these moves, the people who are involved will say, 'This is a great revival.' But the Lord says, 'No, neither is this the great revival but both are steps towards it.'*

I believe his prophecy, whatever is happing now are steps to something coming! Early in the year (April 2021) the Lord gave me the following word.

"I am raising a revival generation in the land. A breed unashamed of the gospel of Christ. A movement ready and willing to go into the deep place to receive a deeper anointing and insight to redigg the old wells of evangelical revival in Great Britain and Northern Ireland."

In Psalm 105, David recounts the history of God's deliverance.

"So God decreed a famine upon Canaan-land, cutting off their food supply. But he had already sent a man ahead of his people to Egypt; it was Joseph, who was sold as a slave. His feet were bruised by strong shackles and his soul was held by iron." vs16-18 (TPT)

When Joseph was seventeen years old, he had two dreams that made his brothers plot his demise. The Lord gave him those dreams, yet God allowed Joseph to pass through hell, why? The answer is found in this history psalm written by David. Joseph was 30 years old when God fulfilled his dreams and was made Governor of Egypt (Gen 41:46). He had to wait for 13 years to see those dreams come true! And for a total of 22 years, he was separated from his family. In Genesis 37:2 when his brothers sold him, Joseph was 17, and as I noted above, he was 30 when his dreams of being the head came through. Remember he interpreted Pharoah's dreams in 41:25-28 as being seven years of abundance followed by seven years of famine. In Genesis 45 when he met his brothers for the first time it was already two years into the second lap of Pharoah's dreams.

"Hurry and go up to my father, and say to him, 'Thus says your son Joseph: "God has made me lord of all Egypt; come down to me, do not tarry. You shall dwell in the land of Goshen, and you shall be near me, you and your children, your children's children, your flock, and your herds, and all that you have. There I will provide for you, lest you and your household, and all that you have, come to poverty; for there are still five years of famine."'

Vs 9-11

So, Joseph was clearly 39 years old at this point. Seven years of abundance have passed, and it is two years into the second round of the pair. It is 9 years into Pharoah's dreams.

I always imagine what went through Joseph's mind for 13 years of waiting for his destiny to come to pass. He might have asked questions like me. "Oh Lord, where are you!"

Normally, a Jewish person could not be deemed to be a man until he is 30, but I believe that wasn't what David was speaking about. Look at that passage again,

"Until the time that his word came to pass,
The word of the Lord tested him."

Until the time that the words of Joseph to his brothers (his dreams) came to pass, God's own plans and His word tested Joseph. Which means the Lord allowed Joseph to go through a school of tests and hard knocks for thirteen whole years. Whew! Do you see it? It took 13 years for the word of the Lord to test, prove and approve Joseph so that he could be mature enough to handle revenge and resentment. And when that period was over, I believe Joseph shouted to himself, "it's time to dream again!"

It is only a person whom God's word has tried and tested that can make the following sincere statement:

"But now, do not therefore be grieved or angry with yourselves because you sold me here; for God sent me before you to preserve life. For these two years the famine has been in the land, and there are still five years in which there will be neither plowing nor harvesting. And God sent me before you to preserve a posterity for you in the earth, and to save your lives by a great deliverance. So now it was not you who sent me here, but God; and He has made me a father to Pharaoh, and lord of all his house, and a ruler throughout all the land of Egypt." Gen 45:5-8

How many of us can say this to the very people who are the architects of our misery? Don't worry guys, he said, I know what you are thinking but it's alright, you did what you did and I'm here because God sent me ahead of you to preserve life. That's powerful! It was easy for him because the word of the Lord tested him, and he submitted to God's wilderness university. The story could have been different. Imagine if it were some of us today. The scene would have been opportunity for personal vendetta. He would have spewed fire and brimstone and certainly invoked "Holy Ghost fire" on his brothers.

I have determined to see God in every experience of my life. When God oversees your life, no incident or encounter is without significance. And when the word of the Lord tests a man, forgiveness is always an outcome.

In my journey as a believer, I have always prayed, "Oh Lord there must be something more!" That has been my war-cry ever since I began to intercede for our dear United Kingdom. There has to be something more. An adage from the Igbo tribe of Nigeria says, *"successful mountain climbers don't take sojourn at the bottom of the climb."* You must keep pushing and going.

Joseph's first dream brought him hatred from his brothers, as if that wasn't enough, he dreamed yet another dream.

"Joseph had a dream, and when he told it to his brothers, they hated him all the more. He said to them, 'listen to this dream I had: we were binding sheaves of grain out in the field when suddenly my sheaf rose and stood upright, while your sheaves gathered around mine and bowed down to it'. His brothers said to him, 'do you intend to reign over us? Will you actually rule us?' And they hated him all the more for his dream and what he had said. Then he had another dream and told it to his brothers. 'Listen,' he said 'I had another dream, and this time; the sun and moon and eleven stars were bowing down to me'."
Genesis. 37:5-9 NIV

You might want to define the word 'dream' differently but permit me to define it in a way most appropriate for the purpose of my discuss. I can say that a dream is an idea or vision that is created in your imagination. It is something that you have wanted very much to be or have for a long time. It is a visionary creation of the imagination, a strong desire, goal, or purpose.

This means that when you conceive or conjure an idea in your mind; when you use your imagination to picture an image of what you want to achieve or become; when you catch a glimpse of what your tomorrow would look like, then you can be said to have a dream.

We know that before a building is erected, the architect sketches a drawing of the intended building on a drawing plain. At times when you look at this drawing you may think that it is a real picture of an already existing building. Well, permit me if I say that the building is already existing in the mind of the architect even though it is yet to be erected in the physical. When the architect is making a sketch on paper, he is trying to let other people see what he has already seen in his inner eyes. He is trying to transfer the house or the structure from his mind to the physical. That is to say that ever before the house is built, even before the foundation is laid; the house has already been in existence in the mind of the architect. No one else sees the house because it has not been built but the architect already knows most of the details, the height, the width, the number of rooms, the roofing pattern, etc. How is that possible? Yes, the architect knows all the details because the building is in his mind. Now, give that piece of land to all of us and notice while every other person is looking at an empty land or a bush, the architect is busy envisioning the position of the front door, the position of the windows, the position of the pillars, and so on.

Your dream is that idea or vision that you have created in your mind of what you want to achieve or accomplish, even though nobody has seen it. It is important also to note that your dream is not a worthy dream if it is not higher, better, or greater than your present circumstance. You must conjure dreams that are superior to your present situation. Your dream must be bigger than you and must scare you and remind you of your continued dependence on God. If this isn't the case, it won't be regarded as dream at all, instead it is retardation. Why waste your time dreaming backwards?

A dream first starts like a suggestion, for example "it will be good if I have a car." "It will be good if I have a university degree" "it will be good if I become an employer of labour" Then the suggestion - when given consideration - becomes a wish, "I want to have a car" "I want to be a university degree holder" "I want to be an employer of labour." Then the wish metamorphoses into a strong desire, and then you set the desire as a goal and begin to work towards it.

When there is a strong desire, and you are working towards actualising your dreams, then that's when I can consider that you have a worthy dream. There is a worthwhile desire, set as a S.M.A.R.T (*specific*-*m*easurable-*a*ttainable-*r*ealistic-*t*imebound) goal, and effort is being made towards achieving them. You know what you want, and you are going for it. You have a clear vision of where you are going, and against all odds you keep going. First, you must know what you want and then with enthusiasm you work towards it.

"If your ax is dull and you don't sharpen it, you have to work harder to use it. It is smarter to plan ahead." Ecclesiastes 10:10 GNT

As far as I am concerned, you may pray, but you must plan and, you must perform. Planning and praying without performing is useless. Performing and planning without praying will yield no eternal and lasting result. Carelessness lets people carry on "as the spirit leads." Listen, grace is not reckless impulsiveness. Successful dreams come about as a result of grace and discipline.

Your vision may not be accomplished in a jiffy, but the important thing is that you are making progress towards it. The Bible says in Galatians Chapter 6 verse 9 *"let us not become weary in doing good for at the proper time we will reap a harvest if we do not give up."*

Focus is Inevitable

If you have got a dream, you must be resolute. You do not just get by and say things like, "wherever the wind blows my boat I'll go." No! Instead, you should position your sail in the direction of your destination. A sailor with a dream does not allow the wind to determine his or her destination rather they use the wind to their advantage by setting sail in such a way that cooperation with the goes in the desired destination. A person with vision is focused; irrespective of challenges, they are not deterred. They don't allow distractions and circumstances to force them away from their stated course. Although he may experience some failures on the way, yet he does not give up. Even when he falls, he gets up and gets going until he sees the desired result. If it means starting all over again, they wouldn't mind, so far as in the end the desired goal is achieved.

We can see the young man Joseph, a typical example of a dreamer in our anchor Bible reference; (Genesis chapter 37). Joseph had a dream and narrated the dream to his brothers, but envy and hatred could not allow his brothers see anything good in his dream. He was only a boy among many big brothers, but he was not intimidated by size; he went ahead to conjure a dream and thereby envisioned himself in a position of authority. This boy Joseph was living under the same roof with his fat, tall, big but visionless brothers but He did not wait for his clueless brothers who had no dream of their own instead he went ahead to grab a dream. We gather from the seventh verse that it is most probable that his brothers were bullies, but I am surprised that he did not allow any of those issues to hinder him from dreaming big, instead he envisioned himself above his present predicaments, above his present handicaps, he envisioned himself excelling in dominion and commanding respect in the nearest future.

His dreams were a total deviance from his prevailing predicaments and handicaps. Now going by our earlier definition of dream, we can say that Joseph created in his imagination a vision of himself on the throne. Yes, he had a strong desire to be in a position of authority in the nearest future, he set a goal of what he wanted to be and purposed in his heart that it must come to pass. As we read on to verse 8, we gather that the hatred they had for him rather aggravated on hearing his dreams. His dream fetched him reprimand, envy, and hatred yet the next verse (verse 9) states that

"and Joseph dreamed yet another dream"

When you read down the following verses you will discover that his later dream was not far from the former which his superiors had earlier suppressed with their antagonism. However, the later dream did not only reaffirm the former dream but also added some levels, in the sense that the sun and the moon (referring to their father and mother) would bow to him.

I might be talking to someone who had had a dream in the past. Perhaps the dream was aborted, truncated, thwarted, shattered, or cut short in one way or the other. Whatever has become of your old dream, you've got to dream yet another dream. In the case of Joseph, whom we are using as a case study, his initial dream was talked down; His brothers wanted to talk him out of his dream. As far as the brothers were concerned, they were trying to talk some sense into him. They believed they were telling him to order, to bring him back to his senses. Alas, their reprimand was quenching the spirit in him. It is possible that those you expect that would encourage and nurture your dream may turn around to be the ones quenching the spirit of your dream. Those who have the wherewithal to support you may be the ones to quench your fiery zeal, thinking that they are talking sense into you. Yes! They may have succeeded in quenching your dream, but I am here to implore you to never give up. There is a solemn call today beckoning on you: it's time to dream again!

Don't Listen to The Naysayers

Not everybody will believe that your dream is possible or achievable, some will see it as an impossible venture, and hence they see no need trying at all. In the case of Joseph, his brothers never believed in his dream. It was to them a folktale. So, they spared no effort in discouraging him by every means. Some may ask you "how can you dream a dream that is bigger than you?" How can a small boy like Joseph come up with 'big-big' dreams like that? Perhaps if the dream was coming from the father or from one of their big brothers or any cream de la crème, they would have managed to believe but not for Joseph, a mere child, a nobody, just emerging from nowhere to dream big dreams and expect everybody to believe and support his dreams. If your dreams are not bigger than you, then you really have no place in the grandstands of greatness.

Furthermore, it is important to know that your dream is idiosyncratically "your" dream and not "their" dream nor "our" dream. Hence you should not expect every other person to accept the dream hook line and sinker without questioning. Even when your dream is eventually understood, no other fellow can be as enthusiastic about it as you.
It is possible that being an immature dreamer, like the young Joseph you lack enough tactics to systematically present your dream to your audience. Perhaps your poor presentation of your dream had raised eyebrows in your audience, please do not give up. Learn your lessons and rise and dream again.

The most unfortunate thing to do is to give up when a dream fails. Yes! My dear reader, I say to you: "dream again"

Yes! Catch another dream. However, if you cannot dream another dream then I implore you to re-dream the earlier dream. Yes, reaffirm it, consolidate it, reinforce it, revive it, fan it into flame. If you have tried your possible best to catch another dream but none is available to you again then there is no problem. Pick up your former dream and examine the reason why it failed. If you can discover why it failed, then automatically you have discovered a clue where to start again.

Permit me one more time to present to you another example of a dreamer. Go with me to the Bible in the book of Luke chapter 19 verses 1 – 10. There it is written about a man called Zacchaeus whose dream was to have a meeting with Jesus. He decided "this great man called Jesus whom everybody is talking about every time and everywhere, I want to meet him face to face". So, he went looking for Jesus. He arrived where Jesus was but there was a problem; the crowd was too much he cannot see Jesus. Now to worsen the matter Zacchaeus was a man of small stature; every other person was bigger than him so he could not even push through to the front to get closer where he could at least have a glance. It was as if his dream was shattered by circumstances beyond his control. Incidentally this man refused to capitulate. Instead, he re-strategized; he inquired and found out where Jesus was going next, went there before any other person, climbed a tree, and waited patiently until Jesus arrived so that from the top of the tree, he could have a clearer view of Jesus. In the end he did not only succeed in seeing Jesus, but Jesus eventually picked interest in him and followed him to his house and spent not just a meeting but fellowship with him. When a man of vision encounters failure he does not capitulate, rather he thinks outside the box and re-strategizes. Whatever had befallen your dream, I want to announce to you that to give up is not the solution rather you have to get up and dream again.

There is another category of people. I remember at some point in my life, I heard the Lord say to me that "it is easier to handle failure than it is success." Some people may stop dreaming new dreams because they consider themselves to have "arrived." They have already achieved their dreams for life. Yes, I know there is fulfillment in achieving your dream. There is a kind of satisfaction, peace of mind, joy or I will say gladness that comes when a dream is fulfilled, when you have successfully actualized your desire and you have succeeded in bringing to limelight the full manifestation of your dreams. However, as good as it is to be celebrated, as good as it is to be applauded for a dream come true, you should never stop dreaming new dreams. Remember that as soon as a person stops growing, they start dying.

As we grow older, many tissues in our body go through atrophy, some people even grow shorter! In the same way anyone who stops dreaming new dreams will begin to depreciate. The tempo of the memory of your exploits will definitely gradually go down with time. Very soon, all your magnificent accomplishments of today will gradually become obsolete and the applause that was initially very high will gradually diminish. Therefore, to remain trendy, you must come up with a new dream.

I believe in that old saying, "if what you did yesterday still appears big in your eyes then you have not done anything today." No matter the height you have attained already there is still a higher height ahead, so why stop here? Why stop dreaming when you can still dream? Why stop dreaming when there are more dreams out there? Whether you have accomplished your initial dream, or your dream failed to accomplish for one reason or the other, it is time to dream again.

Additional copies of this book and other book titles from HENRY OHAKAH are available at most bookshops and from amazon.

For a complete list of titles please email us at:
henryohakah@gmail.com or henryohakah@icloud.com

Spirit Wind Books

Bringing the healing word...touching a dying world!

Other Exciting Books
From Henry Ohakah

Come, Holy Spirit
ISBN:978-34650-0-7
Experience the Holy Spirit as never before in this captivating book about the person and work of the Holy Spirit. You will learn ways that God leads and ways that He doesn't.

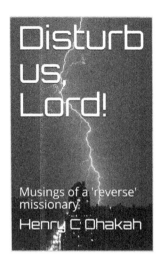

Disturb Us, Lord!
ISBN:9781073518968

Too many churches have a 'Do not disturb' sign hanging on their door. May we be shaken out of our state of slumber and be jolted out of apathetic complacency.

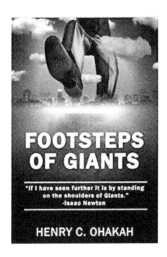

Footsteps of Giants
ISBN: 9781725199170

There are powerful lessons to be learnt from great achievers and successful people in every walk of life, more importantly the giants of the Christian faith. Truth is that they were not lazy, dull, inactive, or idle. They inherited the promises not by wishful thinking but by careful observation and planning.

About the Author

Henry has a background in accounting and finance. He is a Cultural Architect and seeks to bring the Gospel of Jesus Christ to people irrespective of their background and experiences, leaving his accounting profession to respond to God's call of *"bringing the healing word and touching a dying world"* (Matthew 10:7-8). He is a sought-after conference speaker and crusade evangelist and has spoken at churches and large outdoor gospel campaigns in cities across Africa, USA, and Europe.

He releases the glory and power of God everywhere he goes with a strong prophetic anointing with deep insights into the Word of God that motivates you to be successful and rapturable.

Henry is the Senior Pastor of Mexborough Life Church, a modern, vibrant church at the heart of South Yorkshire, United Kingdom and president and founder of Spirit Wind World Impact. In his spare time, he enjoys football, writing and jumping around with his children and his sweetheart, Anita.

Invite Henry to Speak at Your Church or Event

Inviting Rev Henry to come and minister is simple. We work with churches and ministries of all sizes. Henry has preached the Word both locally in England and across the world in places like the USA, Switzerland, and Nigeria, and has conducted open-air gospel campaigns in Togo, Benin Republic, Cameroon, Liberia, and Nigeria. Please let us have these details when you write in. You are under no obligation to book, and the invitation is finalized and scheduled only when the event is confirmed.

Your name and title/position at your church/ministry, email, best phone number to reach you at, name of the church/ministry hosting the event, event location/address, dates & times you want Henry to minister.

Contact Information

Mexborough Life Church
New Oxford Road
Mexborough, S64 0JL
South Yorkshire
UNITED KINGDOM
Phone: +44-1226-234-432
Email: henryohakah@gmail.com

AFRICA
Henry Ohakah Foundation
54 Cameroun Road, PO Box 2721
UMUAHIA, NIGERIA
Phone: +234-802-451-1616
Email: henryohakah@icloud.com

NOTES

NOTES

Printed in Great Britain
by Amazon

79608790R00113